Palgrave Studies in Arab Cinema

Series Editors
Samirah Alkassim
Film and Video Studies
George Mason University
Fairfax, VA, USA

Nezar Andary
College of Humanities and Social Sciences
Zayed University
Abu Dhabi, United Arab Emirates

This series presents new perspectives and intimate analyses of Arab cinema. Providing distinct and unique scholarship, books in the series focus on well-known and new auteurs, historical and contemporary movements, specific films, and significant moments in Arab and North African film history and cultures. The use of multi-disciplinary and documentary methods creates an intimate contact with the diverse cultures and cinematic modes and genres of the Arab world. Primary documents and new interviews with directors and film professionals form a significant part of this series, which views filmmakers as intellectuals in their respective historical, geographic, and cultural contexts. Combining rigorous analysis with material documents and visual evidence, the authors address pertinent issues linking film texts to film studies and other disciplines. In tandem, this series will connect specific books to online access to films and digital material, providing future researchers and students with a hub to explore filmmakers, genres, and subjects in Arab cinema in greater depth, and provoking readers to see new frames of transnational cultures and cinemas.

Series Editors:
Samirah Alkassim is an experimental documentary filmmaker and Assistant Professor of Film Theory at George Mason University. She is the co-editor of the Palgrave Studies in Arab Cinema and her publications include the co-authored book The Cinema of Muhammad Malas (Palgrave, 2018), contributions to Cinema of the Arab World: Contemporary Directions in Theory and Practice (Palgrave, 2020), the Historical Dictionary of Middle Eastern Cinema, 2nd Edition (Rowman and Littlefield, 2020), as well as chapters in Refocus: The Films of Jocelyne Saab (Edinburgh University Press, 2021), Gaza on Screen (forthcoming 2022), and text book Global Horror: Hybridity and Alterity in Transnational Horror Film (Cognella Academic Publishing, forthcoming 2022) which she co-edited with Ziad El-Bayoumi Foty. She is currently writing a book, A Journey of Screens in 21st Century Arab Film and Media (Bloomsbury, forthcoming 2023) and editing a documentary about Jordanian artist Hani Hourani. She holds an MFA in Cinema from San Francisco State University and a BA in English Literature from Oberlin College.

Nezar Andary is Assistant Professor of Film and Literature at Zayed University in the College of Humanities and Sustainability Sciences. He has published literary translations, poetry, and articles on Arab documentary, and researched the relationship of Arab cinema to the recent Arab uprisings. Among his many involvements in Abu Dhabi, he directed a multilingual play for the Abu Dhabi Book Fair and organized an Environmental Documentary Film Series. In addition, he served as Artistic Director for Anasy Documentary Awards in 2010 and Artistic Director for the documentary series Perspectives and Retrospectives in 2013. He holds a PhD from the University of California, Los Angeles and was a Fulbright recipient conducting research in Syria.

Némésis Srour

Bollywood Film Traffic

A History of Hindi Films' Circulation in Beirut, Cairo, and Dubai (1954–2014)

Némésis Srour
Independent Scholar
Paris, France

ISSN 2731-4898 ISSN 2731-4901 (electronic)
Palgrave Studies in Arab Cinema
ISBN 978-3-031-64490-0   ISBN 978-3-031-64491-7 (eBook)
https://doi.org/10.1007/978-3-031-64491-7

© The Editor(s) (if applicable) and The Author(s), under exclusive license to Springer Nature Switzerland AG 2024

This work is subject to copyright. All rights are solely and exclusively licensed by the Publisher, whether the whole or part of the material is concerned, specifically the rights of translation, reprinting, reuse of illustrations, recitation, broadcasting, reproduction on microfilms or in any other physical way, and transmission or information storage and retrieval, electronic adaptation, computer software, or by similar or dissimilar methodology now known or hereafter developed.
The use of general descriptive names, registered names, trademarks, service marks, etc. in this publication does not imply, even in the absence of a specific statement, that such names are exempt from the relevant protective laws and regulations and therefore free for general use.
The publisher, the authors and the editors are safe to assume that the advice and information in this book are believed to be true and accurate at the date of publication. Neither the publisher nor the authors or the editors give a warranty, expressed or implied, with respect to the material contained herein or for any errors or omissions that may have been made. The publisher remains neutral with regard to jurisdictional claims in published maps and institutional affiliations.

Cover illustration: Gordon Sinclair / Alamy Stock Photo

This Palgrave Macmillan imprint is published by the registered company Springer Nature Switzerland AG.
The registered company address is: Gewerbestrasse 11, 6330 Cham, Switzerland

If disposing of this product, please recycle the paper.

To my grandmothers, Hélène and Jeannette

Preface

For the sake of readability, I have chosen to transcribe Hindi and Arabic terms in simplified form, without diacritical marks or accentuation. As far as proper nouns are concerned, I have kept the spelling chosen by my interlocutors when transcribing their surnames and first names into Latin characters. For the sake of consistency, I have always kept the original titles of the films quoted, according to the transcription favored by the Indian production. I mention English titles when the film was distributed internationally at the time of its first appearance in the text.

Throughout this work, I refer to the Bombay film industry. Although the city was renamed Mumbai in 1995 by the Shiv Sena, the Marathi regionalist party at the head of the municipality, my interlocutors continue to refer to the city by its former name. In order to capture their vision, I have preferred to use Bombay. However, I have kept the name Mumbai for official use.

Paris, France   Némésis Srour

ACKNOWLEDGEMENTS

This book is the culmination of my thesis work, and I owe immense gratitude to those who made this journey possible.

First and foremost, I extend my deepest appreciation to my thesis supervisor, Catherine Servan-Schreiber. Working under her guidance was an absolute joy, as I was not only fortunate to benefit from her stimulating and rigorous mentorship but also to be embraced by an academic "family." I wish I could have shared the final outcome of this work with her, as each portrait within these pages is a tribute to the invaluable knowledge she imparted.

My research was made feasible through the funding provided by the NExT—Dynamiques asiatiques program of the PRES Hésam, fieldwork support from the Centre d'Études de l'Inde et de l'Asie du Sud (CEIAS), and the backing of the Île-de-France region's Mobidoc program. My sincere thanks go to these institutions for facilitating my research.

I am immensely grateful for the Francophone thesis prize bestowed upon my thesis work by the Regional Office of the Agence Universitaire de la Francophonie in the Middle East. This recognition encouraged me to transform my research into the form of a book. I would also like to extend my sincere thanks to my editors, Samirah Alkassim and Nezar Andary. I am grateful not only for the opportunity to share my work through this book but also for their editorial choices that consistently aim to broaden understanding and knowledge of Arab cinemas. Their insightful guidance and support throughout the editing process have been invaluable, and I am truly grateful for their belief in this project.

I extend my heartfelt gratitude to the "HESCALE" and "Productions et circulations des biens culturels" research groups, which provided a platform for me to present my work and gain valuable insights from fellow researchers. These groups offered a dynamic and stimulating intellectual space, transcending disciplinary and geographical boundaries.

My research journey also introduced me to fellow enthusiasts of (Indian) cinema, whose academic work and curating work breathe life into films. I extend my heartfelt thanks to all of them.

Through this research, I had the privilege of meeting remarkable individuals whose dedication and passion contribute, often in pioneering ways, to the revival of these films. Whether their names grace the pages of this book or they prefer to remain anonymous, I deeply appreciate their time and the knowledge they shared. These interviews served as a wellspring of inspiration, shedding light on a rarely told story.

A special acknowledgment is reserved for Jocelyne Saab. Her invaluable assistance and generosity were instrumental during my fieldwork in Lebanon, and her own efforts towards promoting Asian cinema in the country are commendable. More than that, discovering her films marked a turning point in my research, inspired by her resolute and vibrant personality.

The fruition of this research owes a great deal to the unwavering support of my parents and my brother. Their encouragement, love, and faith in my work provided serenity during these lengthy years.

Finally, I would like to express my deepest thanks to my partner for his warm presence throughout the process of writing this book.

CONTENTS

1 Introduction 1

Part I Perceptions of Hindi Films in the Middle East: A "Natural" Market Explained by Cultural Affinity 19

2 The Middle East, a "Potentially Rich Market" for Indian Films 21

3 Manchersha B. Bilimoria, Defining the Contours of the Indian Foreign Film Market 29

Part II 1954. Bombay Film Factory, Cairo-centric Circulations: Politics, Movies, Imaginaries 35

4 Cairo 1954: *Aan*, Paving the Way for Hindi Films in Egyptian Cinema Halls 37

5 Bombay 1954: *Chandni Chowk*—Egypt Made in Bollywood 47

6 1954, Dancing the Orient: An "Egyptian Belly-Dancer" in Bombay Studios 57

Part III 1964–1977. The Fabrics of Bollywood: Weaving Films into Trade Routes. Travelling Bombay, Tehran, Beirut   63

7   The Sindhi Film Merchants, Bringing Bollywood to Tehran   65

8   From Tehran to Beirut, the Jumani Brothers   77

9   Bollywood Shoots Beirut, Beirut Screens Bollywood   83

Part IV 1973–2007. Shifting Spaces, Shifting Audiences: Bollywood's Decades of Transition in the Arab World   95

10   Shubra Palace's Hero: Badi' Sobhi, The Distributor That Created Bollywood's Golden Age   97

11   1985, Amitabh Bachchan's *Mard* in Cairo: Embodying a Transnational Masculinity   109

12   Shifting Spaces: From Public Cinema Halls to the Privacy of Homes   117

13   Antoine Zeind, Film Distributor in Egypt, "Why Should I Take Risks and [Distribute] a Bollywood Film?"   131

Part V 2004–2014. Reconfiguration of Cinema Circuits: Rise and Reborn in Dubai   139

14   Ahmad Golchin, The Pioneer: Father of U.A.E Cinema and Indian Film Distributor   141

15   Bollywood, the Diaspora and Dubai's Mediatic Boom: The Renewed Conquest of the Middle East   145

16 2013, Distribution Beyond the Gulf: The *Dhoom 3* Attempt 159

17 When Bollywood Builds Dubai Filmic Imagery: Renewed Visions of the Arabian Peninsula 167

Conclusion 175

Index 179

ABOUT THE AUTHOR

Némésis Srour holds a PhD in Social Anthropology and Ethnology from the École des Hautes Études en Sciences Sociales (EHESS) in Paris. Her research specializes in the film industry, combining historical and ethnographic approaches. She has been honored with a prize from the Agence Universitaire de la Francophonie (AUF) regional office in the Middle East for her research on Bollywood film networks in the region. Alongside her academic work, she has curated Indian and South Asian films in French cinemas, contributing to bringing these cinematographies to light. Additionally, she has taught subjects such as Indian cinema history, international relations, and film exhibition and distribution.

LIST OF FIGURES

Fig. 1.1	Official invitation for the opening of the third edition of the Cultural Resistance International Film Festival of Lebanon in 2015. (Source: Personal Archives)	14
Fig. 7.1	Naaz Building, Bombay. (Source: Personal archives, photo taken in December 2014 in Bombay)	68
Fig. 9.1	Indian Movie Posters from the Collection of 'Aboudi Bou Jawdah. (Source: Personal archives, photos taken in June 2014 in Beirut)	85
Fig. 9.2	*Junglee* (Subodh Mukherji 1961) at Cinema Pigalle (Beirut). (Source: Excerpt from Antoine Kabbabé personal video archives dating back to 1973, Cinema Pigalle (Beirut))	87
Fig. 12.1	The office of Zee at the entrance of Media City in Dubai. (Source: Personal archives, photo taken in June 2014 in Dubai)	122
Fig. 12.2	"We brought Bollywood to Arabia. We are Bollywood." (Source: Personal archives, photo taken in June 2014 in Dubai)	123
Fig. 15.1	Godzilla poster along Sheikh Zayed Road	154
Fig. 15.2	Display of movies screening times inside the cinema	155
Fig. 15.3	Hollywood blockbuster posters in a Dubai mall	155
Fig. 15.4	Hindi film poster inside a cinema in Dubai. (Source: Personal archives, photos taken in May 2014 in Dubai)	156

CHAPTER 1

Introduction

Abstract Among the global audiences for Bollywood cinema, the Arab world is one of the most prominent and the least understood. By examining historical and geographical contexts of film distribution, the book questions the essentialist narratives surrounding Bollywood's Arab audience. It delves into the mechanisms of film circulation—networks, agents, and locations—revealing insights into South-South circuits.

This introductory chapter clarifies key terminology, opting for "Hindi films" over Bollywood or Indian films and emphasizing "circulation" over distribution. It justifies the focus on urban centers like Beirut, Cairo, and Dubai during a postcolonial era, highlighting their significance in the transnational flow of cinematic culture. The chapter clarifies the methodology adopted, a transnational ethnographic approach aligned with New Cinema History methods.

By unpacking these themes and methodologies, this chapter lays the groundwork for a deeper exploration of Bollywood's reception in the Arab world, aiming to contribute to a more nuanced understanding of the dynamics of cultural exchange.

Keywords South–South circulations • Bollywood • Arab World • Ethnography • Transnational • Film circulation

Among the global audiences for Bollywood cinema, the Arab world is one of the most prominent, and the least understood. "Why the Arab World is Infatuated With Bollywood," GQ magazine online promised to explain (Gupta 2022), "Forget Hollywood, Egyptians are in love with Bollywood," was the headline of *The World* an American radio website on May 17, 2015 (Dean 2015). These contemporary news stories reflect the Arab world's long-held love for Hindi films, as historian B. D. Garga testifies:

> Well over a decade after its release in India, the Cinémathèque Algérienne was showing *Mother India* to a packed house. As I watched the film, I was surprised to discover the spell a rural Indian family had cast on a wholly Arab audience. (Chatterjee 2020, 97)

The success of Indian films in Southern locales underscores the resonance that Indian cinema has had in "societies in transition" where "modernity competes with tradition, where urban and rural commingle in uneasy proximity, where underdevelopment meets development"[1] and the creation of "parallel modernities" (Larkin 1997).[2] The ethnographic documenting of cultural global flows of Indian film in the Arab world, shifting the focus away from the screen and towards the film industry backstage, allows to recenter the gaze from the position of postcolonial societies, in order to look beyond the "centrality of the West" (Larkin 1997, 408). Yet, the Arab world's relationship with Hindi films is more ambiguous than it seems, if only we look away from the screen.

In 1965, at a Conference on Arab Cinemas and Cultures, held under the aegis of the UNESCO, the presence of Indian films in the Arab region sparked debate. While some Arab attendees perceived the popularity of Indian films as an "invasion," the reasons for this success were formulated in essentialist terms by the film historian Georges Sadoul, "As far as the importance that Arab countries attach to Indian cinema is concerned, this is a kind of innate spontaneity that I cannot explain" (Centre interarabe du cinéma et de la télévision 1965).

---

[1] Priya Joshi, "Knocking on Heaven's Door: Can Hollywood's Audiences Let Bollywood in?", unpublished paper, cited in Gopal et Moorti (2008, p. 27–28).

[2] On Indian films' appeal in societies in transition and parallel modernities, we can refer to works on Nigeria and Greece: Larkin, Brian. "Indian Films and Nigerian Lovers: Media and the Creation of Parallel Modernities." *Africa: Journal of the International African Institute* 67, no. 3 (1997): 406–40; Eleftheriotis, Dimitris. "'A Cultural Colony of India.'" *South Asian Popular Culture* 4, no. 2 (2006): 101–12.

The popularity of Indian films in Arab countries is often seen as an enigma, compared to the barriers they face in Western countries; at times, critics have accredited its popularity to shared values around the notion of family, modesty, and shared sentimentality. The circulation of Indian films within the Arab world, and the Arab public's love of these flamboyant musical melodramas, are determined and explained in essentialist terms, both by agents from the Western world and by local consumers themselves. The aim of this book could have been to find explanations for this "innate spontaneity," to support the idea of "innate" cultural affinities between India and Arab countries, and to offer a posthumous response to Georges Sadoul by analyzing the film as text. Rather than start from such essentialist cultural explanations, or give arguments within the framework of this system, I will begin by going back to the geographical and historical places where Indian films were distributed. My first step was to look off screen and go beyond film analysis, be it cultural and/or aesthetic, to make use "of other methodologies and other sources than those typically central to film studies," that of "archives, trade magazines, newspapers and oral histories" (Elsaket et al. 2023, 3).

In search of these "nomadic" Indian images, to use Hans Belting's concept (Belting 2011, 21), which have traveled from Bombay to Beirut, Cairo, and Dubai, my research has itself taken an itinerant form to infiltrate these circulations. It followed a nomadic path that had to accommodate the opening and closing of territories, playing with borders and their redefinitions in view of foreign films. In the course of these migrations, images and their status are transformed as they arrive in other spaces. If an Indian film left Bombay as one of the biggest commercial successes of its time, with a star-studded cast of actors and a renowned director, by the time it arrived in Egypt or Lebanon, it was sometimes part of the stream of B-movies confined to second-class cinemas and their popular audiences. Circulation transforms the very value of the film, as well as the modalities of its movement through time. Paradoxically, while contemporary globalization advocates an openness and permeability of borders, my nomadic images come up against barriers that run counter to this supposed fluidity. From these obstacles, Indian films find other circuits and other ways of distribution. The cultural reasons for Hindi films' success in the Arab world have never been truly evaluated, measured, or questioned. The first thing I wanted to do was to clear the ground for the circulation of these nomadic films, to question the process. How do Bollywood films circulate, through which networks, and who are the agents of this diffusion?

Where are the locations of circulation, and what do these locations tell us about the place of this object in the public space?

By examining the processes of circulation of Indian films in the Middle East over a long period of time, from the 1950s to the contemporary era, this work crosses a multitude of histories: that of inventions and technology, a national political history, but also the economic history of the world of film merchants and distribution, as well as the history of migration and the history of piracy. However, before rushing into this protean history, let's make a freeze-frame on the vocabulary that I will use to designate my object, its space, and its modalities of diffusion: the lexical choice of Hindi films instead of Bollywood or Indian films; of Middle East and Arab space, as well as of circulation instead of strict distribution.

Definitions: Bollywood/Indian Cinema/Hindi Films/Bombay Films

There is no such thing as Indian cinema, nor is there an essence to Indian cinema. Indian cinema does not exist because it is plural, multiple, protean. India is home to several film industries, the most prolific of which are the production centers in Bombay/Mumbai, Madras/Chennai, and Calcutta/Kolkata; its cinemas express themselves in more than twenty regional languages; and its films span a wide spectrum of genres, from art films to the big commercial machine, from experimental films to genre films, from independent films to cinema bis. Thus, there has been a plurality since the beginning of cinema in India, a plurality that challenges a singular definition under the aegis of the national prism. The many regional industries—whether Tamil, Bengali, or Marathi—each have their own history and aesthetic tradition.

For the Indian government, there is a clear desire to subsume linguistic and regional diversity under the umbrella of the hegemonic Hindi-language Bombay cinema, the voice of national unity. Although Bombay is located in the state of Maharashtra, whose regional language is Marathi and which also has a long tradition of auteur cinema, this political role of Bombay cinema implies that productions are made in Hindi. Cinema has been seen as the ferment of linguistic unity and as an instrument of nationalist politics in post-independence India. The Hindi-language commercial cinema of Bombay is the one that shines internationally and often condenses the perception of Indian cinemas from abroad. In its pan-Indian vocation and as the standard-bearer of Indian culture abroad, Bombay cinema forms a space of its own. In the words of Indian poet and screenwriter Javed Akhtar, Hindi cinema is a transnational territory in itself:

> There is one more state in this country and that is Hindi cinema ... The culture of Hindi cinema is quite different from Indian culture, but it is not alien to us, we understand it. Hindi cinema is our closest neighbor. It has its own world, its own tradition, its own symbols, its own expressions, its own language and those who are familiar with it understand it. (Akhtar and Kabir 1999, 35)

This cinema, with its nationalist vocation as a tool of soft power, is often called Bollywood. The term has been in use since the 1970s or so, although its origin is a matter of debate. The issue, renewed with each book on Bollywood, is to define and circumscribe the term. For Ashish Rajadhyaksha, the term Bollywood refers to an entire cultural industry, of which Bombay cinema itself is only a small part (Rajadhyaksha 2003). On the other hand, Bombay cinema's international scope has made it a favored cultural export. In this sense, the term Bollywood is usually preferred to support the transnational character of the Bombay film industry: "We use the term Bollywood instead of commercial Hindi cinema to capture the global dimension of this formation" (Kaur and Sinha 2005, 4). Ashish Rajadhyaksha defines it as that which exists and provides primarily for the needs of the Indian diaspora (Rajadhyaksha 2003). Bollywood, through the dominance of its productions in the export of Indian films, is the spearhead of Indian cinemas abroad (Athique 2012, 113). Partly due to Hindi-language films' international potential, capable of rallying both diasporic and non-diasporic networks, as well as its commercial quality, capable of making its mark in both theatrical and festival circuits, this work focuses on the Hindi-language commercial films of the Bombay industry.

However, I will not include these films under the sole label of Bollywood for several reasons. First, I want to give the global phenomenon of Bollywood its local contour. The term Bollywood has become the central concept for talking about the dissemination of Indian films in the contemporary era of globalization, and even of a "Bollywood culture" following a wave of Indian films from the Bombay industry in the 2000s in Europe and the United States. Moreover, the term is closely associated with the diaspora. It is often discussed as, on the one hand, a cultural commodity destined for the Indian diaspora and, on the other, as a space for negotiating Indian identity, between tradition and modernity. Consequently, the concepts that accompany the term Bollywood do not, in my opinion, allow for the specific issues of the circulation of Indian films in the Middle East region in their historical dimension and even tend to narrow the focus. In the course of this work, I will use the term Bollywood to refer exclusively to the popular commercial film productions of the Bombay industry in the Hindi language, and their particular aesthetic style. This style may be marked by visual and sound codes, but this does not mean denying the historical dimension of these codes and the work of transgression and reinvention within Bollywood itself. To designate nomadic Indian films, those that circulate specifically within the Arab space, I will use the term "Hindi film."

My use of the term "Hindi film" can be justified simply: the films that circulate there are essentially Hindi-language films. Secondly, the term "Hindi film," as opposed to Bollywood, seeks to highlight the difficulties of a global reach and circulation of Indian films. Instead of a Bollywood industry that operates within a globalized space, it is a matter of restoring the local, even hyper-local contours of the circulation of these films within the Arab world. Moreover, Bollywood, as a relatively recent notion, tends to obstruct the historical asperities of the Bombay industry in its dissemination abroad. By privileging the term Hindi film, I aim to restore and privilege the study of the disseminations of Indian films in their diachronic dimension. Obviously, it is not new to say that Indian films have been circulating abroad for several decades, but recent studies tend to privilege the contemporary focus, essentially from the 1990s onwards, which marks India's liberal turn and its integration into the globalized world. The term Bollywood tends to restrict our understanding of the phenomenon of the circulation of Indian films, associating it with a cultural commodity destined for the diaspora and contemporary globalization, whereas the notion of "Hindi film" allows me to decompartmentalize these semantic power relations while highlighting the plurality of the modes of distribution of Indian films.

Thirdly, at another level of argumentation, "Hindi film" takes up the category used in the Middle East: as I discovered in the press or during my interviews, the term Bollywood is very rarely used. Taking "Hindi film" as it is, using a phonetic transcription of Arabic for Indian film, emphasizes the semantic origin of the word "India" in which the Arabic language has played a role (Nizami 1994, 54). By using Arabic phonetics to refer to Indian film, it simultaneously transposes Hindi film as a category in itself within the Middle Eastern cultural landscape. "Referring to something as a 'Hindi film' is a way of describing theatrical behavior, probably in reference to the genre's exaggerated fight scenes" (Dean 2015). The very term Hindi film carries a symbolic value and places Indian films in the imagination of Arabic-speaking populations. Thus, the "Hindi film" in this work intrinsically designates the film object originating from Bombay that circulates in the Middle East. But which Middle East are we talking about?

Definitions: Middle East/West Asia/Arab World/ Arab Space

"What happens if we look at the Arabian Peninsula from the South Asian subcontinent instead of from Western universities?" asks Toby C. Jones in an introductory essay "Theorizing the Arabian Peninsula" on jadaliyya. com. To expand on Jones's question, what happens if we look at the Arab world from the South Asian subcontinent instead of from Western universities? Instead of the Arab world, one would encounter Western Asia. The mapping and naming of a territory is a matter of power, a political issue, even more so when these territories exist in a close or distant relationship between the center and its peripheries. The very term Middle East carries with it these power stakes and the place from which it is designated, since the French and British mandates in the region gave it its borders. In contrast to a history of European domination, Nehru's post-independence Indian policy, in line with the Non-Aligned Movement, aims to give full weight to Asia in the perspective of an Indian Asiaticism in which India could take a central place. In this vision of the world, with Asia at its heart, the Middle East becomes Western Asia, as a counterpoint to Eastern Asia, putting India at the center of international geography.

The question of the denomination of the Middle East or Arab World, in all their political and semantic flux, became a lexical issue during my interviews in the field. To clear up this issue, I asked, how the actors of the Bombay industry referred to and perceive this territory? In Indian film industry reports dating from the 1950s onwards, when foreign territories are mentioned, the term used to refer to the region of the Arab world is the Middle East. Often, the terms Middle East and Arab populations function together in the discourse. Therefore, in the field, I have used the category of Middle East in my interviews with my interlocutors, at the expense of the term "Western Asia," which reflects a geostrategic thinking tinged with the discourse of an era and is little used in the world of cinema. In the course of this work, I will articulate the notion of Middle East with that of Arab space, as defined by the anthropologist Franck Mermier. I use the term Middle East to emphasize the perspective of this territory from the vantage point of the Bombay industry, especially to articulate this space as a region of export for Hindi films. At another level, the term Arab space serves as a more general framework for my analysis since, in the wake of Franck Mermier, it allows me to question the notion of the "Arab world," which defines the region as a cultural area and reinforces stereotypical views of this region. The term "Arab space" allows us to decompartmentalize these perceptions. For these reasons, the term Arab space reflects a decentered approach, while insisting on the local differences, from one country to another, within this supposedly unitary cultural area.

Spaces and Chronology: Urban Circulations in Beirut, Cairo, and Dubai in a Postcolonial Period

In terms of chronology, I have chosen to begin my analysis from the time of these countries' independence, in the 1950s. I will then traverse several different nations, discussed below, from the 1960s, '70s, '80s, and '90s, finally ending in the second decade of the twenty-first century. My choice to begin at the moment of decolonization, however, risks obscuring earlier circulations that took place during the colonial era[3] and assumes deviating from the postcolonial frame.[4] My ultimate goal is to propose a perspective unearthing South–South film circulations, embedded from the localities' own perspective and narratives.

---

[3] On colonial film circulations, we can refer to Grimaud, Emmanuel. *Bollywood Film Studio: ou comment les films se font à Bombay*. Paris: CNRS, 2003: 19–48. Thomas, Rosie. *Bombay before Bollywood : Film City Fantasies*. The SUNY Series, Horizons of Cinema. Albany (États-Unis): SUNY Press, 2013. Dwyer, Rachel. "Bollywood's Empire. Indian cinema and the diaspora." In *Routledge Handbook of the South Asian Diaspora*, edited by Joya Chatterji and David A. Washbrook. Londres/New York: Routledge, 2013. Bilimoria, M. B. "Foreign Market for Indian Films." In *Silver Jubilee Souvenir. Indian Talkie (1931–1956)*, by Film Federation of India, 53–56. Bombay: Film Federation of India, 1956.

[4] To expand on moving away from "conventional frameworks" in the Gulf region in particular, see Yunis, Alia, and Dale Hudson. "Introduction: Film and Visual Media in the Gulf." *Middle East Journal of Culture and Communication* 14, no. 1–2 (September 28, 2021): 5–22.

In order to unravel the supposed unity of an Arab world through the lens of Hindi film distribution—since journalistic and promotional discourses generally spoke of Arab populations eager for Indian films—I chose to operate within the more restricted space of Egypt, Lebanon, and Dubai. I have delimited my field of study to these three countries because of their weight and importance in terms of the film industry. Egypt, first of all, because of its long tradition of film production and export in the region; Lebanon, because of the dynamism of the field of exploitation with an audience index that was among the highest in the region (to be modulated according to the periods) and a particularly high ratio of the number of screens to the number of inhabitants. Finally, the Emirate of Dubai, which is emerging as the new regional media center, thereby reconfiguring the geography of cinema within the Arab space. While the national framework serves as a structure for thinking about cultural policies according to each country, I found it more precise to narrow down to three cities: Beirut, Cairo, and Dubai. It's in these cities that one finds the greatest number of cinema screens, and I have chosen them with a view to analyzing the circulation of these films in their urban dimension. Cinema is usually connected to urban leisure practices, leaving aside practices within rural areas, which would be the subject of other types of problematics. This urban focus aims to capture the distribution of Hindi films in their most visible form and to highlight transnational networks rather than circulations within a national space. It highlights "a geographical porosity of cinema circulations and unsettle the frame of 'national cinema'. National frame (…) is inadequate for understanding the sprawling global networks and influences that shaped cinematic cultures in the Arab world" (Elsaket et al. 2023, 5).

By deviating from the "diasporic focus" as an apparatus for understanding the dissemination of Indian films abroad, this work allows us to "decompartmentaliz[e] space and time" (Figeac and Bouneau 2017, 8) and render visible the manifold links that unite India with other regions of the world. Next, I insert my analysis of the circulation of Indian films in a broader history of South–South circulations. Within studies of globalization, which at first focused on North–South relations, South–South circuits are enjoying renewed interest because they offer models for future exchanges. In the case of cinema, South–South circulations are part of a political history that unfolds against the backdrop of the Non-Aligned Movement and the Cold War: "The south-south internationalism of this era was very different in structure and content from the market-driven globalization of the contemporary moment. Hindi popular cinema's reception in 'transitional societies' needs to be distinguished from Bollywood's contemporary cachet in global consumer culture" (Gopal and Moorti 2008, 40). By looking away from the West, the pivotal role of Hindi cinema within a globalized South emerges from this and articulates for scholars "an alternative globalism" (Gopal and Moorti 2008, 7), where the resonance of this cinema "has historically served to negotiate questions of tradition and modernity and continues to inform identity formation" (Gopal and Moorti 2008, 9). For Gopal and Moorti, the editors of *Global Bollywood: travels of Hindi song and dance*, "Bollywood cinema partakes in at least three circuits of globalization: metropolitan, diasporic, and subaltern" (Gopal and Moorti 2008, 6). The examples of our three locations thus integrate urban networks, diasporic networks, and, at a specific moment in history, a "subaltern" audience, a category that allows us to understand the modalities of the golden age of Hindi cinema in Egypt. Thus, the dissemination of Hindi films in the Middle East highlights a history of South–South cinema circuits, at the same time charting a new path through globalization studies.

Transnational History and New Cinema History

Bollywood Film Traffic is at the crossroads of several fields of research that seek to renew perspectives in film history. First of all, my method is in line with the desire to go beyond the framework of the nation-state in writing the history of networks and exchanges of goods, to be part of the vision of a "connected" and "global" history, defined by Sanjay Subrahmanyam as histories "in conversation."

In trying to make this alternative history of trans-regional circulations, I have come up against the sporadic nature of the sources and the conservation of archives in each of the countries involved in these circulations, another form of the underground, invisible dimension of these circulations. What, then, can be said of a history of the films shown in cinemas, when, "the history of the theaters (and/or of their owners) is less easy and locatable than the one of the films" (Forest 1995 introduction, paragraph 13)? In addition to this epistemological challenge, there is the difficulty of tracing the history of a popular cinema, generally "despised" by the elites of Arab countries, who prefer American or European cinema. My email exchange with Mohamed Soueid, a Lebanese film critic, highlights the classic opposition between commercial and arthouse film circuits:

I don't remember that I wrote that much on Indian movies which played in Beirut and other parts of the Middle East. I will look into my personal archives but I don't think I will find precisely what you are looking for. Indian, rather commercial Indian movies were so popular but they weren't received seriously by local critics. Maybe you can find some articles on renowned figure of Indian cinemas, such as Satyajit Ray or Mrinal Sen, but their films weren't distributed in our local cinema circuits.[5]

Soueid's testimony—a prolific journalist, critic, and filmmaker who wrote for *An-nahar* for almost twenty years and is a living memory of Indian films' presence in Lebanon—testifies to the importance of non-written sources to trace a history of the circulation of Indian films in the Middle East. If one follows only the trail of written sources, the presence of Indian films is rendered invisible. A study of the archives of general newspapers such as *L'Orient-le-Jour*, *An-nahar*, and *Al-ahram* only allows us to locate the presence of commercial Indian films in the weekly film program, while more prestigious cinematographies were given in-depth articles and film reviews. In the 1960s, when the film *Sangam* was released in Beirut, there were articles in the cultural pages of *L'Orient-le-Jour* that dealt with Mexican, Spanish, or Japanese cinema, without the Indian case being discussed in any depth. In this case, it seems all the more important to rely on sources other than those produced by elites, and to consider oral testimonies as vital forms of historical documentation.

To analyze the commercial dimensions of film circulation, I have highlighted the stories and portraits of men who forged the routes by which Hindi cinema travelled in the Arab space. Following an anthropological approach, I wanted to restore the history of the circulation of films from the point of view of the actors of this process, and outside the institutional narratives that often puts them aside. While dealing with a poorly documented history, putting life stories, testimonies, even anecdotes at the heart of the methodological process also allows us to make history differently. This method simultaneously underlines the processes of erasure of certain historical phenomena at the same time as it questions the epistemological tools of research. In this sense, in the essential issue of *South Asian Popular Culture*, "Indian Cinema abroad: historiography of transnational cinematic exchanges," the editors Iordanova and Eleftheriotis take this approach to reconstitute little-studied and little recorded flows of circulation:

[5] Mail in date of 21 January 2016.

The present issue of *South Asian Popular Culture* deliberately (and polemically) foregrounds the anecdotal and the testimonial as a necessary means of asserting an overlooked, undocumented and peripheral history. It is our intention to propose (and substantially document) a different historical narrative that runs parallel rather than contradicts the prevailing one. Indian cinema was internationally popular for a significant period, starting in the 1930s and peaking around the 1960s. There were massive exports of Indian films and massive international interest in it. However, as these exports and acclaim did not target (nor took place in) the West (until recently the only place where such processes are properly studied), we really have no record of the intensity of these cinematic exchanges other than sporadic references and anecdotal evidence. (Eleftheriotis and Iordanova 2006, 4:80)

In view of the few sources available, and the difficulties of access, I first traced the circulation of Hindi films towards the Gulf, Cairo, and Beirut. I relied, on the one hand, on written sources such as local press archives (in French, English, or Arabic) and reports from the film and media industry in order to trace the presence of Indian films in the announced programs of cinemas. On the other hand, I have consulted oral sources such as interviews with former and current actors of the circulation of Indian films in the Middle East during field trips to Egypt (April 2014), India (in Bombay, Delhi, Pune, Goa, and Indore, August–October 2013), Lebanon (May 2014 and November 2015), and Dubai (June 2014 and December 2015). Mumbai is an extremely vast terrain when it comes to clearing film distribution: networks stretch from the multiple distributors who now work for integrated groups, the informal distributors, and the government. Identifying the actors and investigating beyond the most visible forms of transnational circulation, namely international distribution companies and media groups, was a significant challenge. The relatively short duration of my fieldwork (for practical reasons of financing) added the disadvantage of having to clear a field in a very short time by identifying both contemporary actors and those of the past, therefore even less visible. The collection of the words of the living to testify to this history had to be combined with archival research in numerous scattered locations.[6]

[6] The National Film Archives of India (NFAI) in Pune, India, offers a beautiful collection of digitized film periodicals, but they are only accessible on site. I only had time to consult a part of it during my stay. Similarly, my research in the Egyptian and Lebanese press archives is dependent on the issues available at the Bibliothèque Nationale de France, and on the gaps in the history of the French and English press in Egypt, for example, following the Suez Canal crisis.

Participant observation allowed me to gather knowledge other than that offered by official discourse. As part of this method, I carried out an assignment as an international sales assistant in the Indian distribution company Yash Raj Films for the Cannes Film Festival over the months of April and May 2015. Director Jocelyne Saab, founder of the short-lived but poignant Cultural Resistance International Film Festival of Lebanon, gave me an insider's look at the programming of independent Indian films in the context of contemporary Lebanon. I worked on the last edition, dated November 2015, where the guest of honor was independent filmmaker Anurag Kashyap (Fig. 1.1). Between his Masterclass for students from the University of Fine Arts (ALBA), the audience's reactions following the screening of his film *Gangs of Wasseypur*, and the reading of the students' writings in the framework of the "Young Critic" competition, I was able to assess the pervasive images of Bollywood and how this film resonated with the aesthetic sensibility of young Beirutis and their cultural referents. At the same time, the development of the association Contre-Courants, dedicated to the promotion and distribution of South Asian films in France, offered me a privileged field. Invited twice (in August 2017 and 2018) to the Locarno Film Festival in the "Open Doors" section (dedicated to South Asian productions for the 2016–2018 season) as a distributor, I was able to meet one of the key people in the circulation of Hindi films in the Middle East. I had been searching for this merchant family for two years already, trying to activate the various networks of Sindh researchers (since this family is a Sindhi merchant family) and my own connections in the industry, without succeeding in making a contact. Finally, the position of distributor allowed me to meet the very actors of these transnational circulations. Moreover, as Contre-Courants distributed its first feature in June 2017, a film from Bangladesh, this also allowed me to acquire practical knowledge about distribution in France, and of the unique issues involved in the distribution of South Asian films, thereby offering a comparative perspective on the circulation of Hindi films in the Middle East.

This work has had to build on gaps and establish the history of circulations at the same time as trying to identify, compile, and make sense of incomplete data on the history of the film industries in India and the Middle East. The existence of in-depth works on the cultural media industries of the region in their historical dimension, including a history of cinemas, exhibitors, distribution and distributors, would have helped to refine the analysis. In the absence of such data, this work is intended to be

Fig. 1.1 Official invitation for the opening of the third edition of the Cultural Resistance International Film Festival of Lebanon in 2015. (Source: Personal Archives)

a first step in documenting the circulation of Hindi films in the Middle East and offer an alternate vision of the Arab space, from the Bombay film industry perspective.

From the perspective of transnational studies, I have also examined how the Bombay industry accommodated the specific issues of each local film industry that I study here. The transnational ethnography of Hindi film circulation networks in Beirut, Cairo, and Dubai revealed different types of networks and their transformation over time and space. The plasticity at work in the formation of the networks contributes to highlighting a shifting geography of cinema in the region, participating simultaneously in the demystification of a homogeneous Arab world that has been taken over, in its entirety, by Indian films. Will studying the modalities of these cinematographic circulations allow us to leave behind an essentialist vision of cultural affinities between countries of the South? Will it help us to decompartmentalize the category of the "South" in order to restore all its depth, ambiguity, and plural heterogeneity? To render all these questions in their historical dimension, the book is organized in chronological sections, with focuses on specific years, to capture circulations in the form of a "close-up" on their highlight moments.

Part I opens in the 1950s, and grounds the debate on the presence of Hindi films in the Middle East in general. Part II is a focus on the year 1954, that marks the advent of the first Hindi film diffusion in Egypt. Part III focuses on merchant's trade routes in the 1960s and 1970s, with Tehran as starting point in 1964 and the distribution of *Sangam* (Raj Kapoor, 1964), and closing in Beirut in 1977, a couple years after the Civil War started. Part IV examines a central period from the 1970s to the contemporary period, marked by multiple transformations: change of audiences, change of circulations modalities, change of cinematic geographies. They concentrate around key dates: 1973 law on Indian films import in Egypt; 1985 Golden Age of Hindi films in Cairo; and 2007, the launch of cable channel Zee Aflam, dedicated to Bollywood movies. And, finally, Part V offers a dive into the recent reconfigurations of Hindi film distribution around Dubai, and the barriers of circulation outside the Emirates, made particularly visible with the distribution of *Dhoom 3* in 2013. The chronological milestone in contemporary times stops in 2014, the year of my last fieldwork in the Middle East. The book chapters are intertwined with interstitial elements, working as a punctuation on the general partition of the text. These interstitial elements are there to give flesh to the unsung agents of the film industry, to save from oblivion, as much as possible, the persons who paved the way for Indian films in the Middle East, as the purpose of this book is not to offer the arguments of a cultural connivance between Indian films and Arab countries but to document the circulation of films, contributing to a global history of South–South cinematographic circuits.

References

Akhtar, Javed, and Nasreen Kabir. 1999. *Talking Films: Conversations on Hindi Cinema with Javed Akhtar*. New Delhi/New York: Oxford University Press.
Athique, Adrian. 2012. *Indian Media. Global Approaches. Global Media and Communication*. Cambridge, UK Malden, MA: Polity Press.
Belting, Hans. 2011. *An Anthropology of Images: Picture, Medium, Body*. Princeton: Princeton University Press.
Centre interarabe du cinéma et de la télévision. 1965. *Cinéma et Cultures Arabes. IVème Conférence de La Table Ronde Organisée Avec l'aide Technique de l'UNESCO*. Liban: Beyrouth.
Chatterjee, Gayatri. 2020. *Mother India*. New edition. BFI Film Classics. London: Bloomsbury on behalf of the British Film Institute.
Dean, Laura. 2015. Forget Hollywood, Egyptians Are in Love with Bollywood. *Public Radio International*, May 17, 2015. https://www.pri.org/stories/2015-05-17/forget-hollywood-egyptians-are-love-bollywood.
Eleftheriotis, Dimitris, and Dina Iordanova, eds. 2006. *Indian Cinema Abroad: Historiography of Transnational Cinematic Exchanges*. South Asian Popular Culture. Vol. 4.2. Oxford: Routledge.
Elsaket, Ifdal, Daniel Biltereyst, and Philippe Meers, eds. 2023. *Cinema in the Arab World. New Histories, New Approaches*. London: Bloomsbury academic.
Figeac, Michel, and Christophe Bouneau, eds. 2017. Circulation, métissage et culture matérielle: XVIe–XXe siècles [actes du colloque, Université de Bordeaux Montaigne et Domaine de Fargues, 14–16 octobre 2015]. Centre d'études des mondes moderne et contemporain. 1 vols. Rencontres 297. Paris: Classiques Garnier.
Forest, Claude. 1995. *Les Dernières Séances: Cent Ans d'exploitation Des Salles de Cinéma. Cinéma et Audiovisuel*. Paris: CNRS Éditions. http://books.openedition.org/editionscnrs/1399.
Gopal, Sangita, and Sujata Moorti, eds. 2008. *Global Bollywood: Travels of Hindi Song and Dance*. Minneapolis (États-Unis): University of Minnesota Press.
Gupta, Nidhi. 2022. Why the Arab World Is Infatuated With Bollywood. *GQ*, May 24, 2022. https://www.gqmiddleeast.com/culture/arab-world-infactuated-bollywood.

Kaur, Raminder, and Ajay J. Sinha. 2005. *Bollyworld Popular Indian Cinema through a Transnational Lens*. New Delhi/Thousand Oaks (Calif. États-Unis): Sage Publications.

Larkin, Brian. 1997. Indian Films and Nigerian Lovers: Media and the Creation of Parallel Modernities. *Africa: Journal of the International African Institute* 67 (3): 406–440.

Nizami, Khaliq Ahmad. 1994. Early Arab Contact with South Asia. *Journal of Islamic Studies* 5 (1): 52–69.

Rajadhyaksha, Ashish. 2003. The 'Bollywoodization' of the Indian Cinema: Cultural Nationalism in a Global Arena. *Inter-Asia Cultural Studies* 4 (1): 25–39.

PART I

Perceptions of Hindi Films in the Middle East: A "Natural" Market Explained by Cultural Affinity

CHAPTER 2

The Middle East, a "Potentially Rich Market" for Indian Films

Abstract During the late 1930s and 1950s, the Middle East emerged as a significant market for Indian cinema, marked by the establishment of distribution offices in Baghdad and growing popularity despite minimal Indian distributor presence. This chapter delves into the perceptions of Indian agents regarding the Middle East as a potentially rich market, examining notions of "cultural affinity" and potential concerns of a "cultural invasion" from the Arab perspective.

By exploring the contrasting dynamics of Indian film distribution in various Arab countries, the chapter offers insights into the complex interplay of cultural exchange, economic interests, and geopolitical factors. It sheds light on how Indian cinema navigated and influenced the cultural landscape of the Middle East during the period from the 1950s to the 1970s.

Through archival research and analysis, this chapter provides a nuanced understanding of the evolving relationships between Indian agents, Arab audiences, and local distributors. Ultimately, it contributes to broader discussions on the history of global cinema circulation.

Keywords Middle East • Iraq • Syria • Indian cinema • Film distributor • Cultural affinity

© The Author(s), under exclusive license to Springer Nature Switzerland AG 2024
N. Srour, *Bollywood Film Traffic*, Palgrave Studies in Arab Cinema, https://doi.org/10.1007/978-3-031-64491-7_2

In 1956, noted film distributor and exhibitor Manchersha B. Bilimoria said that "popular Indian action films were as popular in the city of Baghdad as they were in any first-class cinema in Bombay" (Bilimoria 1956, 53). At the end of the 1930s, the Middle East appeared as a privileged territory for Indian films, as attested by the opening of two offices in Baghdad by Bombay distributors, where films were circulated to the rest of the Middle East from Iraq. By effectively setting up shop in the region, the joint venture of these two Indian companies allowed them to discover a potential market for Indian films in the region.

A Rich Yet Neglected Market

Just because screenings of Hindi films in Baghdad were popular, however, does not mean that such films were a regular and continuous presence on all screens in the region, nor an ongoing prosperity. When an Indian trade mission of goodwill toured the countries of the Middle East (Bahrain, Kuwait, Iraq, Iran, Syria, Lebanon, Turkey, Egypt, Sudan) in 1954–1955, a change occurred for Hindi films in Iraq:

> Some years ago there was a good market for Indian films in Iraq which has, at present, all but vanished. Iraqi importers told the Mission that they had to import Indian films through agents in Egypt and Lebanon who had to be paid large commissions. Besides, only second-rate pictures were available from these sources. (Birla 1955, 26)

At the dawn of the 1950s, the Middle East figured as a sporadic market for Indian films abroad. In 1951, as the Indian Government reports, Pakistan became the first and most important export market for Indian films, despite the many difficulties in circulating prints and repatriating revenues. As for the Middle East region, according to the Government of India: "Some Indian films are shown occasionally to the nationals of Iraq, Iran, the Persian Gulf area and East Africa" (Government of India 1951, 120). From the mid-1950s onwards, the market for Indian films in the Middle East seemed promising. Egypt, Iraq, Syria, and Lebanon were specifically mentioned: "The Indian Goodwill Trade Mission which visited the Middle East countries in 1954–1955 reported that there was considerable scope for developing an export market in Indian films" (Bilimoria 1956, 55). In its report, the Mission states that the possibilities of this market had yet to be explored, "It is no exaggeration to say that Indian film interests have made little or no efforts to exploit the potentially rich market that the countries visited by the Mission have for Indian motion pictures" (Birla 1955, 11). In the 1950s, the Middle East, according to the figures put forward by M. B. Bilimoria, nevertheless represented one of the most flourishing markets for Indian films, despite a weak presence of Indian distributors. In Africa and Southeast Asia, a good film brought in about Rs. 100,000 at the time; in the West Indies, only Rs. 20–25,000; while the Middle East (including Egypt) could bring in Rs. 100–200,000.

The Middle East, and even more so the countries indicated by Bilimoria, is not an area with a large Indian diaspora. How, then, can one explain the commercial success of Hindi films? The answer for Bilimoria is cultural affinity: "The present market for Indian films is largely confined to countries where Indian nationals have settled down in fairly good numbers and/or whose culture and customs bear some affinity to those of India" (Bilimoria 1956, 54). The culturalist argument for the success of the films was probably forged in the 1930s with the circulation of films referred to as the "oriental genre" in early India cinema (Bhaskar and Allen 2009). Also referred to as oriental fantasy films, they loosely draw on Islamicate culture, creating a sense of commonness, in the eyes of the film industry agents of the time, between India's Muslim community and Arab Muslim countries.[1] The distribution and reception of the film *Lal-e-Yaman* (Wadia 1933) is an example of the perception of convergence of Muslim audiences, in India and in the Middle East. Distributed by Bilimoria, like most of the films produced by Wadia Movietone, the film's staging of a world of Islamic culture was

> undoubtedly designed to a considerable extent to appeal to India's large Muslim audiences of the day—although [...] not exclusively so: the aim was to reach a large crossover audience. (Thomas 2013, 84)

However, box office figures, mentioned in the Wadia Movietone House archives, show that the film was especially popular in Bombay and the north of the country, where a significant proportion of the cinema audience was Muslim. In addition, the film earned significant revenues from foreign territories, which amounted to 5% of its overall revenues, a high

---

[1] On the oriental film fantasy genre and its reception in India, see Thomas, Rosie. *Bombay before Bollywood: Film City Fantasies*. The SUNY Series, Horizons of Cinema. Albany (USA): SUNY Press, 2013.

figure for the time. For Rosie Thomas, this commercial success abroad is not unrelated to the Middle East since "it is more than likely that this and other Wadia films played in Baghdad" (Thomas 2013, 84), in particular through Bilimoria.

THE ARGUMENT OF CULTURAL AFFINITY

The Middle Eastern taste for Indian cinema persisted into the 1960s, and appeared to be a source of concern within those countries who equated the success of these films with a "cultural invasion." The subject was so serious that it was part of the recommendations at the end of the third conference of the round table "Arab Cinema and Culture," organized under the auspices of UNESCO, which took place from 26 to 28 October 1964:

> 8. It is recommended to hold the following conferences and seminars during the years 1965–1966:
>
> - In Beirut, in the autumn of 1965, an East-West meeting to study the questions of the projection of Indian films in the Arab countries and the influence of Indian cinema on the relations between the Arab East and the Far East. (Centre interarabe du cinéma et de la télévision 1964, 196)

This question appeared on the agenda of the fourth conference "Arab Cinema and Culture," which took place in Beirut from 25 to 27 October 1965. On this occasion, the entire day of October 26 was dedicated to "Indian cinema & Arab cinema." An Indian delegation, composed of B. D. Garga, film historian and delegate of the Indian government and Indian observers, with the actress Waheeda Rahman, the producer Hiten Chaudhury, and the distributor Gurmuk Singh, was specially dispatched to participate in the discussions. The official purpose of this conference was to see "what lessons Arab cinema can learn from the Indian experience. In particular, how to use the contributions of traditional culture: literature, theater, dance, music to find an original style to Arab cinema" (Centre interarabe du cinéma et de la télévision 1965).

The presentation of the Director of the French Radio and Television Broadcasting Office (Office de radiodiffusion-télévision française ORTF), Pierre Schaeffer, drew quite an essentialist vision of Arab and Indian cinemas. In a few lines, he formulates the idea of a properly "oriental" cinematographic language as opposed to "western" standards: "It would be wrong to align a whole part of the production, in such countries, on the 'standards' of Western production (Centre interarabe du cinéma et de la télévision 1965). The opposition between the "oriental" and "western" film languages stems from literacy as opposed to "a predilection for a direct 'image language'" and a society of leisure against a "need for the cinema [...] to respond in priority to social needs, other than mere leisure." The third and last paradigm comes from the metaphysical relationship to time: on the one hand, a rational system of division of time that defines the cinematographic spectacle in two genres, the short and the long film; on the other hand, "durations of spectacles that are due, either to a different notion of time, or to a more properly oriental rhythm of communication" (Centre interarabe du cinéma et de la télévision 1965). Thus, Pierre Schaeffer's discourse took up essentialist tropisms, making the circulation of films between India and Arab countries look "natural." He adds, however, the need for the "Westerner," to decenter his glance and his system of values in front of these productions: "One must thus be wary of a narrow alignment on an aesthetics, of the kinds, and of the properly Western functions, and to consider that a part of the production of such countries can and must deviate, without falling, of the standards known as international" (Centre interarabe du cinéma et de la télévision 1965). The idea of a community of cultural sensibilities, however, is contradicted by the impossibility of proving the assured success of Hindi films in the Middle Eastern countries concerned.

A Contrasted Presence

In practice, the essentialist views of the west were contradicted by the administrative discourses of Syria and Egypt. In the imagination of the industry's agents, be it Indian or French, the Middle East and its Arab culture were therefore seen as a privileged host country for Hindi films. However, the Middle East is far from being one homogeneous space, and whether one considers Egypt, Jordan, Syria, or Lebanon, the circulation of Indian films is in fact very different depending on the country. First, the report attested to the scarcity of Arab films in India, where some Arab countries had already received Indian films in abundance. The head of the Syrian delegation "admits that his country first witnessed an invasion of Indian film, but this has since been tempered considerably. The black and white films quickly became boring. The color films were quite appreciated if not for the high-pitched voice of the singers. Finally, the historical films went almost unnoticed" (Centre interarabe du cinéma et de la télévision 1965). When the Indian Goodwill Trade Mission visited Syria during December 28–30, 1954, in Damascus and Aleppo, it noted, "There is a very good market for Indian films in Syria. Unfortunately only unsuitable films have so far been shown in that country, until the recent projection of 'Aan' which drew large crowds over a number of weeks" (Birla 1955, 37). Both these statements are consistent with the policy of the Syrian government, which in the early 1960s decided to grant the state a monopoly on film imports in the country. Founded in 1962, the General Organization of Syrian Cinema "had achieved several upheavals in the context of the cinema, and in particular with regard to the import of films, nationalized and provided by governmental bodies" (Centre interarabe du cinéma et de la télévision 1972, 5). Abdel Hamid Merei, Director, detailed the difficulties in controlling the import, highlighting the desire for state control of images: "Films continuing to circulate in the country prevented us from launching the batches of films that we had carefully selected from Western productions" (Centre interarabe du cinéma et de la télévision 1972, 7). In the periodical of the Centre interarabe du cinéma et de la télévision, dated May 15, 1970, the statistics for films imported into Syria mention that 23 Indian films were authorized by the censor and 10 films prohibited (Centre interarabe du cinéma et de la télévision 1970). As of March 15, 1971, censors list 15 Indian films authorized and 8 prohibited, all of them in the private distribution sector (Centre interarabe du cinéma et de la télévision 1971).

On the contrary, the Egyptian delegate "added that he could not give a clear opinion on Indian films, given their very limited number in Egypt" (Centre interarabe du cinéma et de la télévision 1965). Between 1952 and 1963, Egypt is said to have imported 42 Indian films, which represents about 1% of foreign film imports over the period, whereas the United States represent about 75% of imports in terms of number of foreign films. The main countries whose films arrived in Egypt were those of Italy, France, Great Britain, the USSR, Greece, India, the "RFE,"[2] Japan, and Spain—placing India in seventh position out of the nine main countries.

---

[2] Is this a typographical error on the documents and does it refer to West Germany (RFA in French)? However, in the other tables in the appendix of the book edited by Georges Sadoul, *Les cinémas des pays arabes* (1966), the name used is Germany.

This confirms a certain "marginality" of Indian films in Egypt prior to the Six-Day War. UNESCO statistics between 1975 and 1977 show that Indian films continue to be exported to Arab countries, as well as to Africa, Trinidad, Guyana, Barbados, Burma, Hong Kong, Indonesia, Malaysia, Singapore, Sri Lanka, and Thailand.

However, the Arab world, despite UNESCO's desire to highlight Arab culture in the title of the theme of its round tables, cannot be reduced to a homogeneous whole. The heterogeneity of this territory appears in the differing presence of Indian films as well. Each country shares a different bond or history with Hindi films. Even though the UNESCO's enterprise wants to make the South–South or Indian–Arab relationship seem as a natural one, the reconstitution of film circulation in Egypt, Lebanon, and Dubai relates a different history. As a proof, I will demonstrate that Indian distributor Manchersha B. Bilimoria's ability to navigate the differences between Middle Eastern nations and cultures is based on a meticulously constructed knowledge.

REFERENCES

Bhaskar, Ira, and Richard Allen, eds. 2009. *Islamicate Cultures of Bombay Cinema*. New Delhi: Tulika Books.

Bilimoria, M.B. 1956. Foreign Market for Indian Films. In *Silver Jubilee Souvenir. Indian Talkie (1931–1956)*, by Film Federation of India, 53–56. Bombay: Film Federation of India.

Birla, M.P. 1955. *Report Indian Goodwill Trade Mission to the Middle East Countries (1954–1955)*. New Delhi: Government of India, Ministry of Commerce and Industry.

Centre interarabe du cinéma et de la télévision. 1964. *Cinéma et Cultures Arabes. IIIème Conférence de La Table Ronde Organisée Avec l'aide Technique de l'UNESCO*. Beyrouth, Liban.

———. 1965. Cinéma et Cultures Arabes. IVème Conférence de La Table Ronde Organisée Avec l'aide Technique de l'UNESCO. Beyrouth, Liban.

———. 1970. Informations. No. 76 (July).

———. 1971. Informations. No. 90–91 (March).

———. 1972. Informations. No. 122–123 (September).

Government of India. 1951. *Report of the Film Enquiry Committee (1951)*. New Delhi: Government of India, Films Division.

Thomas, Rosie. 2013. *Bombay before Bollywood: Film City Fantasies*. The SUNY Series, Horizons of Cinema. Albany, NY: SUNY Press.

Wadia, J.B.H., dir. 1933. *Lal-e-Yaman*.

CHAPTER 3

Manchersha B. Bilimoria, Defining the Contours of the Indian Foreign Film Market

Abstract This chapter delves into the pioneering role of the Indian film distributor Manchersha B. Bilimoria, a key figure in recognizing the potential of the foreign market and the Middle East for Indian cinema during the first half of the twentieth century. Collaborating with the Wadia brothers in establishing Wadia Movietone, Bilimoria played a crucial role in shaping the landscape of Indian film distribution. Through an exploration of his strategies and insights, the chapter provides a nuanced portrait of Bilimoria as an advocate for the development of overseas markets and sheds light on his unique perspective on the Middle East market. It also critiques the government and film industry's failure to capitalize on international opportunities, as perceived by Bilimoria.

Keywords Portrait • Foreign market • Overseas • Film industry • Middle East • Distribution

The first major entrepreneur to see the importance of the foreign market and the Middle Eastern potential was Manchersha B. Bilimoria. Bilimoria's name appears in Indian history books alongside the Wadia brothers' names. In 1931, the release of the first Indian sound film, *Alam Ara* by Ardeshir Irani, encouraged J. B. H. and Homi Wadia to set up their own studios as well as to start a distribution office for both Indian and foreign films. In 1933, the Wadia brothers established their banner, Wadia Movietone, with the help of Parsi entrepreneurs and industrialists, M. B. Bilimoria and Nadirshaw and Burjorji Tata. Their first association was materialized around the 1933 classic Parsee theater-derived Oriental fantasy film, *Lal-e-Yaman*. The deal is said to have largely been in M. B. Bilimoria's favor, paving the way for India's unique exhibition/distribution system comprising vertical deals with a multitude of small operators.

INDIAN DIASPORA AS "AN INTEGRAL PART OF THE INDIAN MARKET"

In 1956, as President of the Indian Motion Picture Distributors Association, M. B. Bilimoria published a text analyzing international distribution of Indian films, titled "Foreign Market for Indian Films." It is part of a collection of texts on cinema and its industry, mixing aesthetic, social and economic analyses, published on the occasion of the twenty-fifth anniversary of the first Indian talking film. Bilimoria decries the government and film industry's lack of vision to create a real international market for Indian films:

> In the early days of the Talkie, there was little effort to expand the foreign market until about 1935. A good number of Indians lived in the various parts of the British Empire. They always desired to keep in touch with their homeland for which films provided the best medium. But there was no organized machinery to satisfy this demand. Occasionally, a few adventurers came from Singapore or Africa or Trinidad. They had no particular interest in Indian films. To satisfy their trade interest they made enquiries about Indian films and the producers gave them pictures for very nominal amounts. The producers had no idea of gaining a market; neither had the buyers the least inclination to exploit their films in their countries. (Bilimoria 1956, 53)

Bilimoria knew that there was no distribution strategy in releasing Indian films in Indian settlements as a cultural commodity:

> There has always been a demand for Indian films from the large number of Indians who have settled down in Africa, Mauritius, Fiji, Malaya and Singapore, Trinidad and British Guiana. Pakistan, Burma and Ceylon were always treated as a part of the Indian market. (Bilimoria 1956, 53)

For Bilimoria, these circulations do not really represent the overseas market, as they are an "integral part of the Indian market." The challenge for Indian films in terms of international distribution was to enter the American market and compete with Hollywood productions. Bilimoria echoes the desires of his time: "There has been a strong demand for the development of the market in America and Europe both from the Indian film industry as well as from the Government of India" (Bilimoria 1956, 54).

BILIMORIA, AN ADVOCATE FOR THE DEVELOPMENT OF OVERSEAS MARKET FOR INDIAN FILMS

However, Bilimoria pointed to three major obstacles to the foreign market's development. He deplored the neglect of producers, the lack of government support, and the difficulties in importing countries, emphasizing the lack of government support in India. Cinema, reduced to pure entertainment, was despised by the ruling elites, who preferred "educational" cinema for the public good. In this light, the government wanted to control the export of Indian films. Bilimoria reports on the state control over the films suited for international release:

> There appears to be a feeling with Government that only cultural films should be exported to foreign countries. It will be difficult to know precisely what exactly is a cultural film of India. [...] Even though there is no official restrictions on exports, it has been reported that the Indian Consulate and Commercial Attaches are not helpful to the prospective exporters of Indian films to the various countries. While they are prepared to render all possible help for importing any cultural Indian film, they do not seem to be interested in the imports of any other type of films into any foreign country. This view of Government and the Indian Embassies abroad will not help the expansion of a commercial market for Indian films. Even in the case of exports to USSR recommendations are made by the Government of India to the Sovexport Films. (Bilimoria 1956, 55)

M. B. Bilimoria's call for the development of a strategy to gain a foothold in the foreign market was consistent with the 1951 Report, of which S. K. Patil was in charge, which called for the creation of an export company to promote foreign markets. For M. B. Bilimoria,

If the foreign market for Indian films is exploited in an organized and systematic way, the time will not be far off when India can stand abreast of any other country in the popularity of her picture abroad. (Bilimoria 1956, 56)

Bilimoria's strategic vision for the development of foreign markets was based on precise knowledge of the film industry of foreign countries, and more specifically, of Middle Eastern countries.

BILIMORIA, A CONNOISSEUR OF THE MIDDLE EASTERN FILM MARKET

Bilimoria regretted the absence of a collective organization that would allow producers to explore and exploit the foreign market according to a common and continuous strategy, as well as the lack of commercial knowledge of the different countries that make up this foreign market. He gives an eloquent example:

> When a producer is approached for a good film by a prospective buyer, say from Lebanon, he insists that the purchaser should buy ten or twelve of his previous pictures which remain unsold. He does not realize that Lebanon is a very small country. It can consume only five or six Indian films and not ten from one single producer, including those produced by him fifteen or twenty years ago. The producer has to realize that the buyer has the option to secure films from any other producing country of the world. (Bilimoria 1956, 54)

This example is of interest for several reasons. First, it highlights the fine and subtle science of M. B. Bilimoria, who manages to distinguish between the different territories of film export, from the world in general, and from the Middle East in particular. The case mentioned testifies to producers' ignorance of the foreign market and of the competition from other films, as well as of the absence of strategic reflexivity to truly invest in these territories. The prevailing vision, which Bilimoria stigmatizes and identifies as a major obstacle to the development of foreign markets, is that of a simple commercial logic: sell at a good price and get rid of "outdated" or obsolete merchandise in the process. This short-term commercial vision, combined with the presupposition of the Indian government that wished to control the type of films exported abroad, limited the possibilities of exploring and developing the foreign market for Indian films in a fruitful manner. In fact, the first incursions of Hindi films in the Middle East happened in Egypt under a strong political patronage.

REFERENCE

Bilimoria, M.B. 1956. Foreign Market for Indian Films. In *Silver Jubilee Souvenir. Indian Talkie (1931–1956)*, by Film Federation of India, 53–56. Bombay: Film Federation of India.

PART II

1954. Bombay Film Factory, Cairo-centric Circulations: Politics, Movies, Imaginaries

CHAPTER 4

Cairo 1954: *Aan*, Paving the Way for Hindi Films in Egyptian Cinema Halls

Abstract This chapter explores the significant year of 1954 in Cairo, Egypt, when Hindi cinema made its debut in Egyptian theaters with Mehboob Khan's *Aan*. Set against the backdrop of decolonization, the Cold War, and the rise of the Non-Aligned Movement, this period witnessed a burgeoning cultural exchange in the Global South. The close relation between Egyptian leader Nasser and Indian Prime Minister Nehru positioned Cairo as a focal point of Indian foreign policy, paving the way for the introduction of Hindi films to the Middle East.

Examining the political dynamics behind the screening of Hindi films in Egypt, this chapter elucidates the intricate interplay of cultural exchange and political patronage. Through an analysis of the critical reception of *Aan* in 1954, it uncovers the exotic motifs shaping film reception. Beyond print media reception, the chapter delves into the movie theater ecosystem, offering insights into the distribution and exhibition circuits of Egypt and their role in shaping the presence of Hindi cinema in the Egyptian cinematic landscape of the 1950s.

Keywords Egypt • *Aan* • Non-Aligned Movement • Nasser • Nehru • Exhibition circuits

The political repercussions of decolonization, the Cold War, and the rise of the Non-Aligned movement, created "unexpected circuits of cultural exchange in the South" (Gopal and Moorti 2008, 27). In the context of the Cold War, the countries of the South were striving for a new place on the international scene, hoping to impose a "New World Economic Order." Through the close relationship between the Egyptian Nasser and the Indian Nehru, alongside the Yugoslav Tito, the triumvirate led the Non-Aligned Movement, in a policy that effectively placed the Middle East region at the heart of Indian foreign policy. Even more than pro-Arab, Indian policy was "Cairo-centric" at that point in time (Ward 1992), building the space for Hindi films on Alexandria and Cairo's screens.

Egypt and India, a "Cultural" Friendship under Political Patronage

The Bombay film industry of post-independence India was desperate to gain the government's support to explore foreign markets. This was vital for the film industry economic balance as India was largely under-screened compared to the number of films produced. Yet, they would face only contempt from the government who preferred an "educational" cinema for public benefit (Ganti 2012, 47). So, in order to obtain support from the government, for whom the film industry economics was not a convincing argument, cinema owner K. M. Modi argued that the film distribution abroad could be instrumental for India's foreign policy strategy: "I believe that if both Government and the Industry set themselves fully to the task of expanding the foreign market, it will not only help the Industry but also help to foster friendly international relations for us" (Patil 1956, 6). It was in this context of creating diplomatic relations between India and Egypt, relying mostly on the strong friendship between India's Nehru and Egypt's Nasser that the first circulations of Hindi films can be understood.

The political friendship between Egypt and India expanded to various domains, such as economics, education, and culture. Having signed a Trade and Payments agreement in 1953, a special Indian Trade Exhibition was organized in Cairo from April 14 to May 4, 1954. For the local press, this event was an occasion to rekindle the mythology of an ancestral bond between Egypt and India, as an article from April 23, 1954, in the *Egyptian Gazette*, erroneously claimed that Egypt and India had "trade contacts since the time of the Pharaohs" (Egyptian Gazette 1954b, 1). The strong political link and the idea of a community of culture are central rhetorical elements to describe the Indo-Egyptian friendship in the 1950s, even in *al-Kawakib*,[1] a film magazine:

> The ties between Egypt and India have deep roots, permeated by strong political, commercial, and cultural contacts. Recent history is also marked by similar attitudes. When the Egyptian Revolution of 1919 took place under the leadership of Saad Zaghloul, a similar revolution took place in India under Gandhi. When India raised the banner of peace and positive non-alignment in Asia under Nehru, Egypt raised the same banner in the Arab East and the nations of Africa under the leadership of Gamal Abd-al-Nasser. (al-Kawakib, 5 November 1957, quoted in Armbrust 2008, 212)

Besides the commercial agreement, culture was also at the heart of the political friendship, aiming at strengthening "the bonds of brotherhood between two great sister nations," in the words of General Muhammad Naguib, President of Egypt (Le Progrès égyptien 1953, 3).

In March 1953, the India-Egypt Association was created. The Association's work focused on cultural exchange, like literary translation as well as the sponsorship of "goodwill missions, exchanges of professors and students, presentations in Egypt of selected Indian films and vice versa, cultural events, and exhibitions in both Egypt and India" (Le Progrès égyptien 1953, 3). Headed by the illustrious Nawab of Palanpur, popularly known as the "Muslim Maharajah," who was based in Cairo, the Indian Ambassador to Egypt and the Egyptian Ambassador to New Delhi were the Association's honorary presidents. On March 16, 1953, the Nawab of Palanpur addressed the opening ceremony of the India–Egypt association by declaring that the association was "an expression of a spontaneous desire expressed by Egyptian friends of India and Indian friends of Egypt to create an organization suitable for coordinating our cultural and educational activities for the flourishing of mutual friendly relations between Egypt and India." The declaration of friendship was followed by the Indian Prime Minister's message, expressing his joy at this cultural

---

[1] The popular culture magazine *al-Kawakib* (الكواكب) was first published from 1932 to 1934 by Dar al-Hilal, one of the largest and oldest publishing houses in Egypt. From 1934 to 1949, the film section of *al-Kawakib* was integrated into *al-Ithnayn*, the entertainment magazine of Dar al-Hilal. From 1949 onwards, as the film industry developed significantly, *al-Kawakib* was relaunched with film as its main theme (Armbrust 2008, 202).

cooperation: "I am extremely happy to learn of the formation of an India-Egypt Association in Cairo, to which many eminent Egyptian intellectuals and other personalities will belong. In this troubled world of constant clashes and conflicts, it is a good omen that we can think of the arts of peace and ways of cooperation, which after all form the foundation on which the world stands."

Alongside the classical arts such as literature and Indian music— which figured as the essential feature of this inaugural ceremony— and education, there was included one "popular" art form: cinema. The discourse reported by the press reveals two major concerns: the idea of reciprocity in cultural exchanges (the repeated use of the expression "and vice-versa," for example), and that of "selection," denoting a desire for political control over the "arts of peace," according to Nehru's formula.

1954. *AAN*: CRITICAL RECEPTION AND CINEMA CIRCUITS IN CAIRO

Indian films in Egypt benefited from the favorable and willing political rapprochement between the two countries. Yet, *Aan*, the first Hindi film to make it to the Egyptian screens, holds a singular place in the history of Indian film circulation abroad. With a political and sentimental plot, revolving around a king wanting to abolish monarchy and a villager caught in a love triangle between the princess and a girl from his village, Mehboob Khan's production had the stated ambition of bringing this film to international markets. Endorsed by one of India's biggest film studios, since it was the country's first film in Technicolor and directed by one of the most prominent filmmakers, *Aan* generated international distribution on an unprecedented scale for an Indian film, as film historian Gayatri Chatterjee notes (Chatterjee 2002, 10). The Indian film distributor M. B. Bilimoria described the numbers as follows: "It is estimated that today about 15 to 17% of the total revenue of an Indian film is obtained from the foreign markets. In exceptional cases, like *Aan*, this may reach even as high a level as 40% of its total world income" (Bilimoria 1956, 54).

Before arriving on Middle Eastern screens, *Aan* was shown in private circles in London and Paris. In Egypt, the film's premiere took place in a political context, as the opening night of *Aan* was held under the patronage of the Liberation Committee led by then deputy Prime Minister Gamal Abdel Nasser (Le Progrès égyptien 1954a, 5). The film's premiere was attended by members of the Revolutionary Council and the Indian ambassador to Cairo and the proceeds were intended for the Liberation Committee's health fund.[2] Released at the beginning of January 1954, *Aan* found itself in competition on the Egyptian market with Hollywood's first Cinemascope film, *The Robe* (Henry Koster 1953). It nevertheless managed to stay on the screen for six weeks in a Cairo cinema, proof of its great success against its American competitor, which held the top spot for seven consecutive weeks.

The first screening in the Egyptian capital took place on January 7, 1954, at 9:30 pm at the Miami cinema and was released on January 11 simultaneously in two cinemas, Miami and Fémina-Paris. The French press presented it as the first Indian or "Hindu" film. Journalists for the local English and French language newspapers who reviewed the film provided a double perspective on its reception. However, both critics received this film as an exotic and curious aesthetic object. Watching a film coming from Bombay film studios was indeed a first for the English-language journalist, who essentially had no previous knowledge of Indian cinema: "The film *Aan* (showing at the Miami and Femina-Paris cinemas) gives us our first opportunity of seeing what Indian film studios can do" (Egyptian Gazette 1954a). This curiosity also arose in the French-language journal: "This Hindi film was awaited, if not with impatience, at least with curiosity" (Le Progrès égyptien 1954b, 2).

The English review of the film analyses this "first" Indian film's political, technical, and aesthetic aspect. First, critics examined the film's message regarding the organization of a society: "Yet though the film attacks this evil ruler, it does not disapprove of monarchy as a whole, and tries to show that a maharajah can be democratic and popular if he tries." Second, the use of Technicolor: "The most outstanding feature of the film is undoubtedly the colored photography which is so beautiful that it gives one the impression of looking at a series of paintings rather than at an ordinary film." And, finally, from an aesthetic perspective, by emphasizing the songs and dances, the pictorial photography as mentioned before, and the acting: "Filled with Indian songs and dances, the film introduces us to two good actors, the peasant hero and the singing peasant maiden who is full of charm and vivacity."

---

[2] However, this practice was not specific to Indian films, since Nasser also attended the preview of the American film *The Robe* at the Cairo Palace, as reported by the French-language press, whose screening also served as a charity gala.

The French critics, lukewarm and without enthusiasm, insisted on the novel aspect of this film for an audience used to Hollywood imagery, almost defining it as a form of "counter-Orientalism": "Favorable comments given the special character of this film which for the first time takes us into a new environment and introduces us to a setting that only the distorting mirror of Hollywood had presented to us, embellished by the imagination of the scriptwriters?" The film's cultural and aesthetic exoticism make it difficult for the journalist to define. On the one hand, he situates it in a fairy-tale exoticism; on the other hand, he presents it as a film that aims to re-establish the "distorting mirror of Hollywood" and therefore has a "realistic" purpose. The "curiosity" about this exotic object is already apparent in the director's misspelled name, which changes from Mehboob to Mesrob in the French-language newspaper. From the outset, the film is intended to awaken childlike feelings, thus delegitimizing the Indian work at first sight, and placing it below the categories of American and European films. Eventually, in the critic's closing sentence, the film is reduced to the technical quality of the panoramic screen of the Miami cinema, which was specially purchased for the occasion: "*Aan* is a must-see film … especially for the wonderful panoramic screen that the Miami has provided for the screening of this film." Both film critics' expressions denote the exotic reception of this film coming from India, as it is described as a cultural commodity rather than a filmic object.

However, the journalist's perspective did not prevent the local success of *Aan* in Egypt. To go beyond the reception of the film in the written press, we need to understand the movie theater ecosystem in which the film was screened. Looking at the distribution and exhibition circuits of Egypt opens a new perspective on the presence of Hindi films in the Egyptian cinematographic landscape in the 1950s. In Cairo, *Aan* screened at the Fémina-Paris and Miami cinemas, both owned by Solly V. Bianco. Each cinema had its own programming specialty, thereby attracting different audiences. On the one hand, the Fémina was a first-class cinema and was historically the venue for French films.[3] Located at 13 Emad-el-Dine Street, "the street of Arab films," the Fémina, "named Capitole in the 1930s—only showed French films distributed by Pathé" (Bénard 2016,

---

[3] The number of cinemas in Egypt, whether first, second, or third category, is organized according to a hierarchical classification whose main distinguishing criterion is the price of the ticket. This material criterion is based on the geographical location of the cinema and its programming. The first category cinemas are located in downtown Cairo and screen Hollywood, French, or Italian films for the most part.

81). Georges Calothy, a spectator, confirms that, in the 1950s, the Fémina specialized in French films. There, he discovered *Nous irons à Paris*, directed by Jean Boyer (1950), a film that marked his generation. Similarly, the testimony of the actor Omar Sharif describes the atmosphere of this cinema: "I used to see all the French films that were shown at the Fémina. The cinema was small, you had to go downstairs. It was the only well-attended cinema on Emad-el-Dine Street, the others were second-class cinemas" (Bénard 2016, 109). The Miami cinema, on the other hand, specialized in Arab and Egyptian films. Located at 38 Soliman-Pacha Street (Talaat Harb), it was also a downtown cinema, and yet remained an "expensive" cinema, as the taxi in Khaled al-Khamissi's novel of the same name points out, where the price of a seat was up to 16.5 piasters until the early 1980s.

The screening of *Aan* in both cinemas with different programming tones reveals the ambivalent status of the first Hindi film in the Cairo cinematic landscape. In a way, it highlights the difficulty that Solly V. Bianco had in situating this film: did *Aan* belong to the "prestigious" category of foreign film, in the French, Italian, or American film space, or was it to be considered closer to the local Egyptian films? Moreover, the copy of the film had French subtitles, according to the announcement in the daily newspaper *The Egyptian Gazette*, without specifying whether the film had a dubbed copy in Arabic or not. This practice is consistent with that of the Arabic film, which was also subtitled in French, for the audience of foreign residents in Egypt, especially Italians and Greeks, as recounted by director Kamal el-Sheikh (Bénard 2016, 77). Therefore, during its six-week run in Cairo, we can assume that the screenings were primarily aimed at a local elite located in the city center. Yet, *Aan* was not the only film screened at that time. Following the film's success, the year 1955 saw a peak in the number of Indian films shown in Egyptian cinemas. More than the numbers of Indian films imported into Egypt per se, it is the modalities of screening that will show the popularity and place of Hindi films in Egyptian society.

After 1954, the Onset of a First-Class Cinema Circuit for Hindi Films in Egypt

In the 1950s, the reputation of Hindi films benefited from the prestigious movie theaters in which they were screened. Based on interviews, it is possible to identify the particular importance of one film in the imaginations of the local population, building on the prestige associated with the cinema hall where it was screened. A variety of films were screened, be it the most impressive commercial productions of the time like *Baiju Bawra* (Vijay Bhatt, 1952), which was screened for nine weeks in Egypt, at least in the first-class cinema circuit, and *Awara* (Raj Kapoor 1951), to realist films, such as *Do Bigha Zamin* (Bimal Roy 1953), screened for only three days, as well as oriental fantasy films, like *Saqi* (H. S. Rawail, 1952). Yet, the films that were preserved in the audiences' imaginaries, were closely linked to the glamor of the cinema hall in which they were screened.

The importance or popularity of Hindi films in Egypt should not be measured in their quantity or length of screen time only; the cinema halls screening the films should be taken into account as well, as an indication of their place in the public and filmic landscape of the time. One monument of Hindi cinema that is remembered by Egyptians is *Mother India* by Mehboob Khan (1957). Distributed by Wajih Skandar, an Egyptian distributor of Hindi films, it appeared, alongside *Sangam* (Raj Kapoor, 1964), as the Indian film of reference in the popular imagination. Wajih Skandar seems to be one of the first distributors of Indian films in Egypt. He may have passed through the distributor Gurmuk Singh, based in Beirut until the 1970s, who began his career in distribution in the region with the films *Aan* and *Mother India*, while taking over the distribution of lesser-known films (Centre interarabe du cinéma et de la télévision 1965). *Mother India* circulated in an Arabic-dubbed version that, as Safaa al-Leithy, a film editor and critic interviewed by Viola Shafik, an expert on Egyptian cinema, recalls, was screened in a first-class cinema, Metro, in downtown Cairo. "Ironically," Shafik adds, "this cinema used to be reserved for American films before it was nationalized in 1963 along with the country's major studios" (Iordanova 2006, 133). The Metro Theatre, "the Pride of the East," has a special prestige and marks the history of movie theaters in Egypt:

The inauguration of the Metro Goldwyn Mayer cinema in Cairo, known as the Metro, on February 2, 1940, was a milestone. It was remarkable for its rich decor, air conditioning, and large leather seats, all of which had never been seen before; it presented a quality of picture and sound that no theater had ever rendered before, and it offered the public refined service and treatment equal to the sophistication of independent theaters owned by foreigners. It presented (and continues to present), on Friday mornings—the weekly day off—screenings for children, and in the afternoons of the same day, films for the educated cinephile. By any standard, it was the first film club in Egyptian history, a giant film library with old and new films, augmented by a parallel film library of 16 mm films for amateur buyers and constantly adding new prints to maintain its reputation (Mahfouz 1995, 126).

For producer and director Henri Barakat, this cinema was still one of the best in the city in the early 1990s, and for director Youssef Chahine it remains shrouded in a mystical aura:

The Metro theatre in Cairo was so beautiful that it was frightening. One entered it as if it were a temple, with the respect imposed by the red carpets and the uniforms of the staff. This cinema was huge, all wood, before it burned down during the great Cairo fire. After 1952, the woodwork on the walls was not restored. Of course, one could not smoke, eat pips, or throw anything on the ground. It was a far cry from those messy rooms, real stables, like today. (Bénard 2016, 88)

This cinema hall was exclusively reserved for American productions and had a reputation for quality, as noted by the scriptwriter Ahmed Qassem (Bénard 2016, 133). By contrast, Arab films were considered to be bad quality, so the only Arab productions shown at the Metro cinema featured the most famous directors of the time: Henri Barakat, Kamal el-Sheikh, and in particular *Saladin* (1963) by Youssef Chahine. The city center was the space of the local elite and foreign residents, as the actor Nour el-Cherif recounts: "I, who only left my neighborhood during the holiday season, can say that the city center was very clean because it was not very frequented, only by foreigners and the wealthy. The others did not dare to come out of their holes" (Bénard 2016, 154). Alongside these prestigious films, an Indian film, *Mother India*, got to be screened at the Metro, making it part of a sort of pantheon of great films.

Nourished by political ties and foreign policy strategy, the diffusion of Indian films in first-class cinemas in Cairo's bourgeois city center benefited from the political rapprochement between Nasser and Nehru, which paved the way for Hindi film circulations in Egypt. Yet, one may wonder how the political rapprochement may have impacted the images produced in film studios, and the imagination associated to Egypt. Strikingly, at the same period, Bollywood film studios were experiencing an "Egyptomania" phase. In 1954, several Hindi films had Egypt as their background. The next chapter explores the representations of Egypt's filmic stereotypes against the endeavor of filmmaker B. R. Chopra to craft a realistic Egypt in Bombay film studios.

References

Armbrust, Walter. 2008. The Ubiquitous Nonpresence of India. Peripheral Visions from Egyptian Popular Culture. In *Global Bollywood: Travels of Hindi Song and Dance*, ed. Sangita Gopal and Sujata Moorti, NED-New edition, 200–220. University of Minnesota Press.

Bénard, Marie-Claude. 2016. *La sortie au cinéma: palaces et ciné-jardins d'Égypte (1930–1980)*. Parcours méditerranéens. Marseille: Éditions Parenthèses MMSH.

Bilimoria, M. B. 1956. "Foreign Market for Indian Films." In *Silver Jubilee Souvenir. Indian Talkie (1931–1956)*, by Film Federation of India, 53–56. Bombay: Film Federation of India.

Centre interarabe du cinéma et de la télévision. 1965. *Cinéma et Cultures Arabes. IVème Conférence de La Table Ronde Organisée Avec l'aide Technique de l'UNESCO*. Beyrouth, Liban.

Chatterjee, Gayatri. 2002. *Mother India*. BFI Film Classics. Londres: British Film Institute.

Egyptian Gazette. 1954a. The Film 'Aan'... *Egyptian Gazette*, January 17, 1954.

———. 1954b. Commerce Helps Bind Egypt to India. *Egyptian Gazette*, April 23, 1954.

Ganti, Tejaswini. 2012. *Producing Bollywood: Inside the Contemporary Hindi Film Industry*. Durham (États-Unis): Duke University Press.

Gopal, Sangita, and Sujata Moorti, eds. 2008. *Global Bollywood: Travels of Hindi Song and Dance*. Minneapolis (États-Unis): University of Minnesota Press.

Iordanova, Dina. 2006. Indian Cinema's Global Reach. *South Asian Popular Culture* 4 (2): 113–140.

Le Progrès égyptien. 1953. Une Belle Manifestation d'amitié Indo-Égyptienne. *Le Progrès Égyptien*, March 17, 1953.

———. 1954a. Superproduction En Technicolor Flamboyant. *Le Progrès Égyptien*, January 1, 1954.

———. 1954b. 'AAN' Un Film Hindou de MESROB. *Le Progrès Égyptien*, January 12, 1954.

Mahfouz, Medhat. 1995. Les Salles de Projection Dans l'industrie Cinémato graphique. In *Égypte, 100 Ans de Cinéma*, ed. Magda Wassef, 124–129. Paris: Éd. Plume: Institut du monde arabe.

Patil, S. K. 1956. The Year in Retrospect. An Annual Survey of the Film Industry by Leading Spokesmen. *Filmfare*, March 16, 1956.

Ward, Richard Edmund. 1992. *India's pro-Arab Policy: A Study in Continuity*. New York; Westport, CT, Londres: Praeger.

CHAPTER 5

Bombay 1954: *Chandni Chowk*—Egypt Made in Bollywood

Abstract This chapter explores the representation of Egypt in Bombay cinema in the pivotal year of 1954. Against the backdrop of global fascination with Egypt, fueled by the archaeological discovery of the tomb of Kheops, Bombay cinema embarked on its own exploration of the land of the Pharaohs. The chapter examines how Bombay cinema constructs its cinematic Egypt, departing from traditional Orientalist motifs prevalent in European and Hollywood films.

Focusing on the film *Chandni Chowk* by B. R. Chopra, a Muslim social set in both Delhi and Cairo, this chapter argues that it creates a visual narrative that establishes a common Islamicate world between the two cities. While drawing on the visual grammar of Bombay cinema, *Chandni Chowk* moves beyond mere inspiration from the Arabian Nights, offering a nuanced and realist portrayal of Egypt that contrasts with Oriental film fantasies. Additionally, the chapter highlights how Cairo in *Chandni Chowk* embodies a form of familiar exoticism unique to Bombay cinema, diverging from Hollywood's orientalism.

Keywords *Chandni Chowk* • B. R. Chopra • Egyptomania • Islamicate World • Muslim Social • Hollywood

© The Author(s), under exclusive license to Springer Nature Switzerland AG 2024
N. Srour, *Bollywood Film Traffic*, Palgrave Studies in Arab Cinema, https://doi.org/10.1007/978-3-031-64491-7_5

In 1954, the archaeological discovery of the tomb of Kheops triggered a frenzy for Egypt. From Hollywood to Bollywood, the cinematographic landscape was fascinated by the land of the Pharaohs. In Hollywood, within a year, Michael Curtiz's *The Egyptian* produced by Fox; Howard Hawks' *Land of the Pharaohs* financed by Warner and touted as having "all the grandeur and pomp of ancient Egypt";[1] and Robert Pirosh's *Valley of the Kings*, set out to capture the Nilotic atmosphere in its own way. At the same time in 1954 Bombay, the Bharat Jyoti Films company was shooting its *Cleopatra*, while the films *Naaz* (S. K. Ojha) and *Chandni Chowk* (B. R. Chopra), with Egypt as their backdrop, were released.

CINEMATIC ORIENTALISM: EUROPE AND HOLLYWOOD PICTURING EGYPT

In the American and European imaginations, Egypt occupies a singular place as the "gateway to the East," the passage to India for Europe and Great Britain in particular.

> That Egypt was both a Christian and Muslim country, with a history of pharaonic religions as well, contributed to its status as a point of interchange between, Europe and Africa, the Middle East, and beyond. Richard White writes of this 'ambiguity' of Egypt along similar lines, noting that while it was 'indisputable part of the Orient, the Orient being less a place in the East than part of a discourse in the West,' it was not easily placed within Africa or Asia, or within the East or the West. (Lant 1997, 79)

European cinema appropriated the Egyptian world—already present in a whole visual tradition that drew on the motifs of Egyptology (Lant 1997, 76)—by including it in fictional scenes, both contemporary and historical, or in newsreels shot on location even before the First World War. Whether in biblical films shot in studios, or in natural settings in Egypt, or in the surge of mummy films in the United States, Egypt occupied the Western cinematographic imagination very early on. With the advent of synchronous sound, however, "the power of the silent Egyptian past over cinema had disintegrated (or at least went underground)" (Lant 1997, 93). In the spring of 1954, when films depicting the ancient Roman Empire were inspiring Hollywood, an archaeological discovery directed

---

[1] *Le Progrès égyptien*, November 7, 1955, p. 3.

film producers' attention to the other side of the ancient Mediterranean, to Egypt. The arrival of CinemaScope contributed to the visual rhetoric of the "ancient" film. At a time when the American majors were looking for a solution to bring the public back to theaters, the HyperGonar invented in 1927 by the Frenchman Henri Chretien appeared to be the solution to the drastic drop in spectators in the United States. Renamed CinemaScope on January 29, 1953, the French system was, according to Darryl Zanuck, "the Fox's savior" (Mannoni 2016, 216). *The Robe* (Henry Koster), a biblical film, was the first Scope film projected by Fox, whose technology became the new standard of cinema while deploying the imaginary of the antique film in spectacular fashion. In the rhetoric of American films, the representation of Egypt takes up motifs, as described by Ella Shohat:

> Through a historiographical gesture, the films define the Orient as ancient and mysterious, participating in what Derrida in another context calls the 'hieroglyphist prejudice'. The cinematic Orient, then, is best epitomized by an iconography of Papyruses, Sphinxes, and Mummies, whose existence and revival depend on the 'look' and 'reading' of the Westerner. (Quoted by Nashef 2013, 201)

Images of Egypt engraved within filmic imaginaries draw upon the symbolism set by Hollywood, so much so that "[t]o our preconditioned modern eyes, so conditioned since 1908, an 'ancient' film often needs the pictorial splendor and broad scope in order to look 'ancient'" (Solomon 2001, 19).

While Hollywood has vastly imposed its orientalist imagery of Egypt, the representation of Egypt in Bombay films studios attempts to depict an Orient created by the Orient, to quote the title of François Pouillon & Jean-Claude Vatin's book (Pouillon and Vatin 2011) and draws upon an alternative set of exotic imaginaries. B. R. Chopra used neither the pyramids nor the Nile in his visual grammar of the country, thus questioning the specificities of the Bombay filmic vision of Egypt. At the crossroads, B. R. Chopra's film *Chandni Chowk* recycles an Orientalist visual imagery by using some symbols of ancient Egypt, but above all, offers a modern and alternative vision of the country of the Nile.

Chandni Chowk, a Muslim Social in Delhi and Cairo: Visual Rhetoric of a Common Islamicate World

In 1954, two Hindi films propose a rather antagonistic vision of Egypt. The first one, *Naaz*, which we can only judge through a review in *Filmfare* magazine, borrows from the codes of the oriental fantasy film, a genre of films inspired by the *One Thousand and One Nights* tales (Thomas 2013):

> The romance sets in when the son becomes a stoker on an ocean liner and is smitten by the charms of the lovely Princess Nilima. Follow some absurd and incredible scenes aboard the liner, including a fancy dress ball which must be seen to be believed, a fantastic engine room revolt, a farcical fire and the liner's wreck, from which only the stoker and the Princess survive to find themselves on the Egyptian shore. How they get from there to the Sphinx is nobody's business apparently. But they do, warming up for love in the desert heat because by the time the Sphinx cooks upon them they are well in the torrid zone and put over some scorching love scenes in a pool which grows conveniently right there in the sand complete with oyster shells embedded in its banks. The music is pleasing and the songs are well sung. The dances are poor and the hybrid numbers are out of place in Egypt, land of the renowned 'Danse du Ventre'. (*Filmfare* 1954b, 23)

To resume, *Naaz* is a story about a princess, taking place in the desert, and with belly-dance sequences: these same elements—apart from the Sphinx, an icon of a defined locality—are used indifferently to picture any exotic Oriental world.

B. R. Chopra's *Chandni Chowk*, on the other hand, is a different kind of film, belonging to the genre of the Muslim social, part of the larger vein of *Islamicate cultures of Bombay cinema*, as theorized by authors Bhaskar and Allen (2009). As they argue, "the Islamicate imagery popularized by the Orientalist fantasy films did not disappear; rather, it was integrated into representations of the cultural and expressive traditions of the Muslim elite" (Bhaskar and Allen 2009, 7). The Bombay films' concept of "Islamicate cultures" refers, in this sense, to the social and cultural system historically associated with Islam and Muslim communities, both among Muslim populations themselves and among non-Muslim communities (Bhaskar and Allen 2009, 3). This Islamicate culture, defined by narrative motifs drawing on Persian narratives, poetic forms such as *ghazal* or singing traditions such as *qawwali*, infuses Hindi cinema as a whole.[2] In these Hindi films, cities like Agra and Lucknow personify the urban Islamic imagination. The architecture of these cities is mobilized in Islamic films in general through the use of easily recognizable and iconic locations such as the Agra Fort, Akbar's city at Fatehpur Sikri, or the Taj Mahal. These places and monuments anchor the narrative in a real geographical space and simultaneously operate on a symbolic level, signifying a nostalgic space of Muslim grandeur.

"In the process, the Islamicate idiom in the cinema of the Silent period was also identified with imagined geographical spaces of the larger Islamic world, thus giving an actual if diffused sense of location to the cinematic fantasies of the beyond" (Bhaskar and Allen 2009, 5). One of the visual conventions of Bombay cinema, for example, is the use of domes and minarets to represent Arab cities. The films thus show a more global Islamic spatial form through the use of three main elements that were introduced into Indian architecture with the arrival of the Muslims in South Asia—as seen in the monuments of the Sultanate period, long before the grandiose monuments of the Mughals: the minaret, the dome, and the Islamic arch. "The use of these elements in the mise-en-scene signaled an Islamicate world even the monuments were not so easily identifiable, and they were readily replicated in studio sets or models" (Bhaskar and Allen 2009, 11). The Islamic arch could take a variety of forms: pointed, horseshoe-shaped or horseshoe-headed, an arch in the form of a brace, or scalloped. This central element was combined with colonnades and arcades with round, scalloped roofs, balconies with serrated trellises in palace interiors, terraces supported by pillars with trellis walls and serrated backs, and the terraced and landscaped gardens for which Muslim rulers were famous. By borrowing and assimilating a common visual grammar between Indian Muslim culture and Arab space, Bombay cinema weaves a red thread between this geographical space and the Muslim community. In so doing, it contributes to staging a filiation that constructs the Muslim community as exogenous to the Indian space.

This same process is applied in the film *Chandni Chowk*, where a sense of symmetry is created between Delhi and Cairo by introducing each city in a similar way. An opening intertitle sets the space and time of the film:

---

[2] On the place of Muslim myths within the Indian cinematic corpus, see Azevedo, Amandine d'. *Mythes, Films, Bazar.* Illustrated edition. Sesto San Giovanni: Mimesis, 2018, 218–229.

Delhi in the early twenties, while the opening credits take place against a backdrop of multiple views of the Jama Masjid in the political capital. The intertitle locating the action at the beginning of the film is answered by the intertitle, in the middle of the film, which signals the displacement in another geographical space in Latin characters, in Devanagari (for Hindi) and in Arabic script (for Urdu) (following a common practice of Bombay cinema): Egypt (misr in Hindi and Urdu, i.e., the Arabic name for Egypt for the latter two), against a backdrop of Islamicate architectural views. The similarity of the process to present the two countries weaves a continuity between the two geographical spaces. Moreover, Akbar's journey to Cairo takes place exactly in the middle of the film, thus splitting it between India and Egypt almost equally and putting both countries on the same plane. In Delhi, the film takes place in a Muslim environment, and the visual syntax operates in such a way as to weave an identity link between Indian Muslims and the Arab world. B. R. Chopra uses the architectural Islamicate motifs in the settings of his film, both when the action takes place in India and when it is set in Cairo, creating a stylistic and aesthetic universe common to both geographical spaces.

The views chosen in the background to present Egypt fade in low houses, the round roofs of mosques and their minarets, a sphinx—symbol-emblem of the country. These elements operate as signifiers of Egypt, drawing on the reservoir of the popular imagination of the Arab world as a land of Islam. However, B. R. Chopra also draws from the cultural history of the subcontinent, borrowing from the reservoir of images of Islamicate culture films. The use of essentialized Islamic architectural motifs in the film *Chandni Chowk* participates in a form of deterritorialization of Cairo with its local and singular specificities within the larger space of the Arab-Eastern world, without real existence.

With its mosques, its mausoleums, its public fountains, its Koranic schools, its caravanserais, and its princely houses, Cairo was one of the jewels of Islamic art. However, apart from the Sphinx, the Egyptian city is not represented through real monuments of its architecture. Al-Azhar for example, a mosque inseparable from Cairo which was built in 970–971, one year after the foundation of the city in 969 by the Fatimid dynasty, Shiite Ismaili, does not appear in our Hindi film, nor the famous mausoleums Al-Husayn or Zaynab. Instead, it is the general Islamic architecture that serves as a representational motif for the city of Cairo: domes and minarets, round and low roofs. To the imaginary of an ancient and desert world is superimposed the motifs of Islam, signified through the architecture and the sets of the films that condense the Muslim world with the imaginary of the Arabian Nights.

> Cairo, in fact, is not only the capital of Egypt, but that of all Nilotic Islam. It is in medieval Cairo that several tales of the *Thousand and One Nights* take place. (Mayeur-Jaouen 1996, 116)

In the mouth of an Ibn Khaldûn in the Mamluk period, the description of Cairo strangely echoes the cinematographic motifs for representing the Arab-Muslim universe of Hindi films:

> Whoever has not seen Cairo does not know the greatness of Islam. It is the metropolis of the universe, the garden of the world, the anthill of the human race, the portico of Islam, the throne of royalty: it is a city embellished with castles and palaces, adorned with convents and dervishes and colleges, illuminated by the moons and stars of erudition. (Quoted by Mayeur-Jaouen 1996)

Rather than these magnificent sights, it is instead the generic Islamic architecture that serves as a representational motif for the city of Cairo: domes and minarets, round and low roofs. The very narrative construction of the film thus establishes a continuity between the Delhi and Cairo, built up as a common Islamicate space.

"AFTER ORIENTALISM"[3]? CAIRO IN *CHANDNI CHOWK*, REALISM AND FAMILIAR EXOTICISM

Even though *Chadni Chowk* built on the Islamicate culture's visual grammar of Bombay cinema, it still goes beyond a depiction inspired by the *Arabian Nights*. In its own way, it re-creates, re-configures and re-defines what would be a realist image of Egypt, in contrast with Oriental film fantasies. In fact, in terms of style, B. R. Chopra is recognized as a commercial filmmaker who "shares with the New Wave of directors, alongside whom he works, a powerful social conscience and a realistic impulse" (Bhaskar and Allen 2009, xi).

---

[3] Pouillon, François, et Jean-Claude Vatin. *After Orientalism. Http://Journals.Openedition.Org/Lectures*. Brill. Visited on July 22, 2023. https://journals.openedition.org/lectures/17824.

B. R. Chopra opens his film by setting it in a realistic time and place, as displayed in the introductory intertitle: "In Delhi of the early twenties the old order was still singing of the past glory." In addition, the precise geographical delimitation given by the film's title, Chandni Chowk, which corresponds to a district of the city of Delhi, attests to the director's desire for a sense of realism. It stands in contrast with the fictional claim of films in the Oriental fantasy genre. The film *Saqi* (1952), a Talwar Films production by director H. S. Rawail, for instance, uses the following metatext in the opening of the film:

> This is a wholly fictitious story and the characters and costumes are not entirely in conformity with the culture and traditions of Iraq. The references to Hindustan and Shahzada Hindustan are totally imaginary and as such have nothing to do with any period of the history of India.

From there, the viewer follows the trials and tribulations of an urban bourgeois family man who falls victim to a farce plotted by acquaintances who find him a little too full of himself: he had almost married off his daughter Zarina, played by Meena Kumari, to the gardener, Akbar (Shekhar), if he had not discovered the subterfuge in time. Zarina, however, considers herself Akbar's wife and goes to live with her in-laws. Akbar then decides to go and make his fortune in Egypt. Once at his destination, the viewer follows Akbar through an arcaded street of bearded men wearing djellabas and tarbouches, until he enters the "Cairo Café." Yet, for a film critic of the time, *Chandni Chowk* presents precisely all the evidence of realism:

> A very realistic set, purporting to be an Egyptian coffee house, complete with smoke-filled rooms, knee-high tables, charming cigarette girls and exotic Bedouins dancers, was created recently at Central Studios for the last few sequences of Hira Films' "Chandni Chowk", now being directed by B.R. Chopra. (Filmfare 1954a, 41)

Overall, the "Egyptian" sequences signal the geographical location of Cairo through signs in the heart of the film's settings or of intertitles inserted in the editing, both as a meticulous attention to realistic details and as a written redundancy of visual signifiers drawing from popular imagination, such as the Sphinx. This redoubling, which aims to affirm and reaffirm the film's geographical positioning in Egypt and Cairo in particular, invites at the same time a form of awareness at the potential ambiguity in cinematic motifs such as sets or costumes between the Arab world and the Muslim community in India. The insistence on preventing ambiguity in the reading of the geographical space of the action reveals at the same time the permeability and circulation of visual symbols of the Indian and Arab Muslim worlds in the filmmaker's perception. Egypt exists and takes shape on the Indian screen only through a minimalist symbolism, without using the multiple potential referents that more distinctly evoke the country in the popular (perhaps more specifically Western) imagination, such as, in a stereotypical way, the Nile, the mummies, the pyramids, or the camels and the desert. In *Chandni Chowk*, Cairo embodies a form of familiar exoticism.

REFERENCES

Bhaskar, Ira, and Richard Allen, eds. 2009. *Islamicate Cultures of Bombay Cinema*. New Delhi: Tulika Books.
Filmfare. 1954a. Filmfare. *Filmfare*, April 2, 1954.
———. 1954b. Chaotic Story Mars S.K. Films' 'Naaz.' August 20, 1954.
Lant, Antonia. 1997. The Curse of the Pharaoh, or How Cinema Contracted Egyptomania. In *Visions of the East: Orientalism in Film*, ed. Matthew Bernstein and Gaylyn Studlar, 69–98. New Brunswick (Canada): Rutgers University Press.
Mannoni, Laurent. 2016. *La machine cinéma: de Méliès à la 3D [exposition, Paris, Cinémathèque française, 5 octobre 2016–29 janvier 2017]*. Edited by Cinémathèque française. Paris: Cinémathèque française.
Mayeur-Jaouen, Catherine. 1996. Coupoles et Minarets d'Egypte. In *Lieux d'Islam: Cultes et Cultures de l'Afrique à Java*, ed. Mohammad Ali Amir-Moezzi. Monde, Hors-Série 91/92. Paris: Autrement.
Nashef, Hania A. M. 2013. Barbaric Space. Portrayal of Arab Lands in Hollywood Films. In *Popular Culture in the Middle East and North Africa: A Postcolonial Outlook*, ed. Munirat Sulayman and Walid al-Hamamsi. Routledge Research in Postcolonial Literatures 46. New York: Routledge.
Pouillon, François, and Jean-Claude Vatin, eds. 2011. *Après l'orientalisme: l'Orient créé par l'Orient. Terres et gens d'Islam*. Paris: IISMM-Karthala.
Solomon, Jon. 2001. *The Ancient World in the Cinema*. New Haven, CT, Etats-Unis d'Amérique: Yale University Press.
Thomas, Rosie. 2013. *Bombay before Bollywood: Film City Fantasies*. The SUNY Series, Horizons of Cinema. Albany, NY: SUNY Press.

CHAPTER 6

1954, Dancing the Orient: An "Egyptian Belly-Dancer" in Bombay Studios

Abstract In 1954, as Egyptian sharqi dancer Nadia Gamal toured India and Sri Lanka, Indian actress Smriti Biswas filmed a belly dance sequence for B. R. Chopra's *Chandni Chowk*. While press archives mention the presence of Egyptian dancers in India and Indian films being shot in Cairo, the influence of Egyptian dancers on Bombay's belly dance sequences remains underexplored. This chapter delves into this intriguing aspect of Bombay cinema.

Exploring the iconic figure of the belly dancer through the lens of Bombay cinema, this chapter traces the historical roots and definition of belly dance before analyzing the dance sequence featuring Indian actress Smriti Biswas in *Chandni Chowk*. B. R. Chopra skillfully blends exoticism with cultural familiarity, offering a nuanced depiction that balances elements of orientalism with film notes of realism.

Keywords *Chandni Chowk* • B. R. Chopra • Belly dance • Bombay cinema • Smriti Biswas • Nadia Gamal

At the very same moment that the Egyptian *sharqi* dancer Nadia Gamal was on tour in India and Sri Lanka, reputedly shooting a film, and meeting with Indian film actors, such as Shammi Kapoor, the Indian actress Smriti

Biswas was shooting a belly dance sequence for B.R. Chopra's film set in Cairo, *Chandni Chowk*. Press archives from the 1950s mention the circulation of the Egyptian dancer in India, and the shooting of the Indian film, *Naaz*, in Cairo. Little is said, however, about the actual influence of Egyptian dancers on belly-dance sequences in the Bombay film industry. We are left with scarce images and information, and yet, the realism of B. R. Chopra's film testifies to the fascination of the time for Egypt and its belly dance.

Does Belly Dance Really Exist? History and Definitions

Used to refer to a generic dance from the East, the term "oriental dance" actually includes very diverse practices. Researchers specialized in this field prefer, for instance, the term "Arab-Berber dance from the Maghreb to the Mashrek," using a more geopolitical categorization.[1] The term *danse du ventre* appeared in France at the end of the nineteenth century, and then circulated in the Anglo-Saxon world under the term "belly dance." It was then reappropriated in Egypt under the name *raqs el-batn*, a literal translation of belly dance, but was eventually abandoned due to its lack of success locally. There are also the names of *kuch-kuchi* or *hoochi-hoochi*, but these terms connote the oriental dance as a form of striptease. In the Arab world itself, there are various names that cover different forms of dance. Thus, *raqs baladi* refers to the traditional form, while *raqs sharqi* refers to a more sophisticated form that arrived with Egyptian cinema; *raqs shaabi* refers to popular dances. When the oriental dance number appears in Hindi film scripts that have the Arab world as a fictional background, film critics refer to it as the sequence of a "Bedouin dancer," suggesting yet another category. This term insists more on the register of a folkloric tradition of this dance, and on the association of the Arab space with the nomadic tribes that populate the Arabian Peninsula.

In the specific cases of oriental dance in Hindi films, I have some evidence about belly dance drawing inspiration from Egypt, based on press archives. The scarcity of historical evidence concerning dance exchanges between Egypt and India as far as the film industry is concerned leaves us with few materials to build upon. However, it is interesting to note that,

---

[1] On this theme, see the colloquium "Le 'corps oriental'. Genre, gestes & regards," December 7–9, 2017, Paris, Université Paris Diderot & EHESS.

in 1954, there is a reciprocal interest around Egypt, India, and dance in the film industry, as two articles point out. The first article from the local Egyptian press mentions the tour of the dancer Nadia Gamal in India and Sri Lanka: "He who has drunk of the water of the Nile ... will drink it. And who was born on the banks of the Nile ... cannot but return to it! After a triumphant trip to Ceylon and India, 'our' Nadia Gamal came back to us very happy to be back in her native land. (...) she really made the Egyptian dance proud."² As the article outlines a circulation of Egyptian oriental dance in India, it also mentions the involvement of Nadia Gamal in a local film production, depicting Egypt. Along with the article, there is a picture of Nadia Gamal with the following caption: "In India, Nadia was in a film where a clever set depicts the Pyramids and the Sphinx in the background." I could not find any evidence of this movie, yet it gives us a sense of the influence of Egyptian imaginaries in Hindi films around 1954.

The second article focuses on the shooting of the dance sequence in *Chandni Chowk* (B. R. Chopra, 1954) and recounts the Indian actress's unsparing efforts to slip into the skin of an Egyptian dancer, to the point of losing weight in the process.

Smriti Sweats it Out
After just three days' work in *Chandni Chowk*, the plump-checked, buxom Smriti Biswas lost three pounds in weight. How? "It was the constant steam-bath I was subjected to", moaned Smriti. It seems that director B. R. Chopra, striving to create an air of mystery for Smriti's dancing scene had the set filled with dense smoke, the doors and windows were shut and no fans were allowed to be switched on. Smriti, heavily costumed as an Egyptian belly-dancer, perspired from head to toe and after three days of steam-bathing lost a little weight. Her fiancé Narang, a former medical student, comforted her, saying: "At least this experience has revealed to you a sure method for slimming. Now you can reduce whenever you want to."
[caption: The gorgeous Smriti, practicing her hot Egyptian dance number for the Hira Films banner's *Chandni Chowk*, slims down without shedding a tear].³

The focus on the actress's body and physical exertion highlights the effort of embodying an Egyptian belly dancer in its most truthful character, emphasizing the sought-for realism of the scene, as well as,

---

² *Le Progrès égyptien*, February 16, 1954.
³ *Filmfare*, August 20, 1954.

paradoxically, insisting on the otherness of it, its exotic dimension. Be it through the body or with music, B. R. Chopra creates, in this sequence, a combination of exoticism and cultural familiarity.

CHANDNI CHOWK IS BELLY DANCING: AN INDIAN ACTRESS AS AN EGYPTIAN DANCER

When Akbar, the young male protagonist of *Chandni Chowk* arrives in Cairo, he enters the Cairo Café, the hypnotic space of an oriental cabaret, where men smoke the hookah and where performs a mysterious belly dancer. Opening to the sounds of tambourine, the sequence operates on three levels: music, song, and dance. The music operates in two modes: it deterritorializes the images by setting up a musical "oriental atmosphere" and it reterritorializes the danced sequence with the belly dancer singing in Hindi.

First, Egypt is "musicked" in the oriental way, according to Gregory D. Booth's concept:

> By musicked, I mean the active construction or reinforcement of identity by means of musical content, performance or other association. In this sense, musicking requires that sounds be understood to have symbolic or semiotical potential. (Booth 2007, 318)

In this oriental "musicalization," the important thing is not to respect the Arab instruments and melodies but to *signify* the Orient through music, even if it uses a detour through the way Hollywood has tuned it. Then, when the dance number starts, the music changes and proceeds on another register. It aims, on the contrary, to attenuate the feeling of exoticism of the images by the use of a familiar music. This disjunctive process, where the sound and the place of the action do not match, is used for the majority of the musical sequences in Bollywood. Set in an exotic location, these sequences are often danced to familiar rhythms (Booth 2007, 325–26).

At the same time, the feeling of exoticism is attenuated by the use of familiar music. If the image shows Cairo, the music and song means India. The tambourine that sounds at the beginning of the sequence serves as a symbolic instrument of the Oriental dancer, while her dance can hardly be recognized as a typical *sharqi* dance. In general, "Once established in the public imagination, the term 'belly dance' was adopted by natives and non-natives to denote all solo dance forms from Morocco to Uzbekistan that engage the hips, torso, arms and hands in undulations, shimmies, circles and spirals" (Shay and Sellers-Young 2005, 1). Thus, the belly dance choreography in the film *Chandni Chowk* focuses on what gives the feeling of a belly dance: the movement of the arms, hips, and a play with the veil. While this dance number may not be convincing in comparison to dance sequences in Egyptian films, this film by B. R. Chopra does stand out from the world of Oriental fantasy films to which the oriental locale is usually confined. It offers yet a more subtle version of the Oriental dancer in a sequence that offers a definition of what is perceived as Egyptian reality.

Part II illustrated the reciprocal filmic interest between Egypt and India in the 1950s, be it with Hindi film distribution in Egypt and imaginaries of Egypt in Hindi productions. The Egyptian case illustrates one typology of networks: the link between distribution channels, politics, and geopolitical ties. The typology of networks established is not intended to be a strict, hermetic categorization. Rather, it highlights a dominant modality, the one that most visibly structures these circulations in a given space. Another typology of circulations of Hindi films is their inclusion in earlier commercial and trade exchanges between Bombay and the Middle East. Films took routes that have already been mapped out through the intermediary of merchant families. Although their role may have been founding and pioneering in opening new circuits for Hindi films, they are not recognized figures in the history of Indian cinema. Part III focuses on a specific merchant family, aiming to bring to light a dimension of transnational history of Hindi cinema mostly left in the shadows.

REFERENCES

Booth, Gregory D. 2007. Musicking the Other: Orientalism in the Hindi Cinema. In *Music and Orientalism in the British Empire (1780s–1940s): Portrayal of the East*, edited by Martin Clayton and Bennett Zon, 315–35. Music in Nineteenth-Century Britain. Aldershot (Grande-Bretagne): Ashgate.

Shay, Anthony, and Barbara Sellers-Young, eds. 2005. *Belly Dance: Orientalism, Transnationalism, and Harem Fantasy*. 1 vols. Bibliotheca Iranica 6. Costa Mesa (U.S.A.): Mazda.

PART III

1964–1977. The Fabrics of Bollywood: Weaving Films into Trade Routes. Travelling Bombay, Tehran, Beirut

CHAPTER 7

The Sindhi Film Merchants, Bringing Bollywood to Tehran

Abstract This chapter sheds light on the transnational dynamics of film circulation, focusing on the pivotal role of a Sindhi merchant family in bringing Bollywood to Tehran. The chapter redefines the history of film circuits, emphasizing the creativity of agents who facilitated film circulation.

Highlighting the significance of Indian merchants as film agents, the chapter traces their crucial role in the early days of the Indian film industry's development. It explores how global trade networks facilitated the transnational circulation of films, transcending national boundaries and mediating connections between local and global markets.

Examining the unique position of Sindhi merchants in facilitating Hindi film distribution, the chapter illustrates their contribution to merchant exchange between India and the Arab world. It unravels the geography of film circulation, starting from Iran and extending to Arabic-speaking countries. The chapter culminates in an analysis of the distribution of Raj Kapoor's *Sangam* in 1964 by the Hinduja family, underscoring Tehran's nodal role in the broader Middle Eastern circulation of Indian films.

Keywords Sindhi Merchants • *Sangam* • Raj Kapoor • Hinduja Family • Tehran • Global Trade

© The Author(s), under exclusive license to Springer Nature Switzerland AG 2024
N. Srour, *Bollywood Film Traffic*, Palgrave Studies in Arab Cinema, https://doi.org/10.1007/978-3-031-64491-7_7

The versatility and lability of film circuits fabricated by a Sindhi merchant family sheds light on the transnational dynamics of film circulations, beyond diaspora circuits. At once a scientific invention and mass cultural product, the early cinematograph has struggled to find its place among the great classical arts. The obsession with legitimizing cinema as an art form (Banda and Moure 2008) contributes to denigrating its industrial aspect and economic dimension. Revisiting the history of film circuits puts the creativity of the agents who materially circulate films at the heart of the matter, rather than artistic creations and aesthetic forms. Such agents harness the intelligence of networks and the capacity to create itineraries and new geographies from established and/or shifting anchor points.

Indian Merchants as Film Agents

In the early days of the Indian film industry, merchants were essential agents in the construction of an industry in the making. However, their instability, their chaotic organization, and the high failure rate of their enterprises are seen as the many flaws of this "stammering" industry by the Indian government, bothered by this uncontrollable creative regime. In 1938, an association of producers published the *Indian Cinematograph Year Book* (*ICYB*) to pay tribute to all the pioneers of cinema in the territory. However, "instead of looking for a founding father, it re-establishes the work of intermediaries and praises these jack-of-all-trades who had been able to distribute films, screen them, multiply production projects and learn to use a camera" (Grimaud 2003, 43). "In this history made by the pioneers themselves, they celebrate the 'circuits-which-are-made-and-are-made-again'" (Grimaud 2003, 43) as a distinctive quality of film networks. The report praises the owner of Krishna Studios as "a symbol of enterprise and experimentation, a shrewd dealer, a prolific producer, and an ingenious screenwriter." Far from pitting art and industry against each other, the "*ICYB* celebrates artistic talent and merchant intuition on the same continuum (Grimaud 2003, 45)".

In the early days of cinema, the circuits were dominated by versatile personalities, who sometimes combined the aspects of merchant-producer-cameraman, where mobility was an intrinsic quality of the image maker. We thus find the figure of the exploitant-nomad in France, which withers with the rental system imposed by Charles Pathé in 1907: he no longer sells the reels of his films to the showmen who used to own them but only delivers his films for rental, arguing that this trade is in decline. In making this decision, Charles Pathé inaugurated the film distribution business. In fact, "the history of distribution is the history of a business in which the intermediary is not a simple economic agent interposed between a manufacturer and retailers, but an entrepreneur who interferes, upstream, in the conception of the film and who, downstream, ensures the best conditions for its sale" (Garçon 2006, 6). In addition to this commercial history, the distributor has the primordial role of organizing the filmic space since he elaborates, builds, and determines the geography of the film's circuits. At Naaz, the distributor's building in Bombay (Fig. 7.1), distribution is based on a territorial division between primary and secondary distributors, and on the trade of an object with an inherent circulatory dimension (Grimaud 2003, 431). To take up the notion defended by the *IYBC*: "The 'meaning of cinema', it is explained, consists in knowing how to die and be reborn again and again in a more solid manner elsewhere, hence the high mortality rate of production companies. This indicates less a fragility of the network than the path it has followed to constitute itself, by spreading itself" (Grimaud 2003, 45).

Going beyond film circulations in India itself, the particularity of global trade networks will help us construct another history of the transnational circulation of films, where the local connects to the global, without having been manifestly mediated by the national (Markovits 2000, 29), as may have been the case in the distribution of Hindi films in Egypt in the 1950s. Because of the very structure of this network, where trade could take place without necessarily drawing up a written contract for each transaction or where private archives are not easily accessible and because of the nature of the places where films were screened—in private spaces in the absence of real cinemas in the Gulf for several decades—I will focus on a global understanding of these exchange dynamics, replacing film circulation between India and the Middle East as part of trade routes.

SINDHI MERCHANTS IN THE MIDDLE EAST: A CENTURIES-OLD TRADE ROUTE

The singular place of Sindhi merchants in the trade and distribution of Hindi films is part of the overall history of merchant exchange between India and the Arab world. "The Arab traders came to the sea coasts of India and carried Indian goods to European markets by way of Egypt and Syria. Thus it was through their merchants that India and Arabia came to

Fig. 7.1 Naaz Building, Bombay. (Source: Personal archives, photo taken in December 2014 in Bombay)

know each other" (Nizami 1994, 53). For Khaliq Ahmad Nizami, the merchant relationship is a structuring aspect of the cultural history between South Asia and the Arab space: "It is against the background of this cultural contact brought about by commercial and navigation needs that Arab contact with South Asia should be viewed" (Nizami 1994, 54). More specifically, "Sindh, as the coastal region of the subcontinent closest to the Persian Gulf, has always been actively involved in maritime trade with that region of Asia. It has also played an important role as a commercial gateway between Central Asia and northern India. Thus both sea and land routes contributed to its commercial importance" (Markovits 2000, 33–34).

We know little about the groups involved in maritime trade in medieval Sindh: both Arab and Sindhi merchants played an important role, without any particular community being identified. It is only from the fifteenth century onward that mention of the merchant caste, the Banians of Sindh, appears in the Arabic and Portuguese documents of the time concerning Muscat. The city of Thatta in Sindh is mentioned as Muscat's main trading partner, and its Hindu merchants, the Bhatias, seem to have been the main participants in this trade between Sindh and Arabia (Markovits 2000, 34). During the period 1750–1843, the Bhatia merchants remained an important trading community in the Persian Gulf and in particular occupied a predominant role in the pearl trade centered on Bahrain (Markovits 2000, 38). Sindh's historical trade links with the Arabian Peninsula and the Middle East make Sindhi merchants fine specialists of the region, combining fine geographical knowledge with commercial knowledge. A Sindhi merchant family invested in the field of cinema, turning into a pivotal structure in the circulation of Hindi films in the Middle East. The geography of this circulation was first organized from Iran and then extended to Arabic-speaking countries.

1964: *SANGAM* AND THE HINDUJA—FROM BOMBAY TO TEHRAN

Hindi cinema is far from being a stranger to Iranian soil, as the two countries have cinematic ties—beyond their connected history—very early in the history of cinema. The birth of Iranian talking pictures was under Indian auspices, since the first Iranian talking picture, *Dokhtare Lor* (Irani and Sepenta 1932) was shot in India, in the studios of the director-producer Ardeshir Irani,[1] from the Indian Parsi community. Abdul Hossein Sepenta shot his film in the Imperial Film Company studios, with an Indian crew and even Indian actors who did not speak a word of Persian: "the technicians were all Indians. I was," says the director, "happy to be working in a big studio with the best technicians in India" (Zeiny 2015, 42). The Iranian director, who had been in India since 1927, had trained in film in Calcutta with the prestigious Bengali director Debaki Bose as his mentor. Sepenta not only benefited from the technical infrastructure offered in Bombay, but the situation in Iran was "catastrophic" and cruelly lacked "the infrastructure necessary for a national cinematography" (Thoraval 2000, 25). However, he was also inspired by Indian cinema in aesthetic terms. He inaugurated song-and-dance sequences in Iranian films, establishing a long aesthetic tradition in commercial cinema (Zeiny 2015, 43). In addition, the Imperial Film Company also produced three Persian films for the Iranian market (Barnouw and Krishnaswamy 1963, 102). Hindi films also circulated in Iran, starting in the 1930s. Their popularity increased with time until they became the first competitors of Iranian cinema in the 1950s. Films such as *Awara* (Kapoor 1951), *Mother India* (Khan 1957), *Pyaasa* (Dutt 1957), *Kagaaz Ke Phool* (Dutt 1959), *Barsaat* (Kapoor 1949), and *Andaaz* (Khan 1949) were great popular successes in Iran (Zeiny 2015, 61). In 1961, an internal memo from the Indian government to the film industry reports a regular presence of Indian films on Iranian screens: "There are approximately 30 cinema halls in Tehran, the capital of Iran, out of which 20 show Indian films either regularly or occasionally" (Barnouw and Krishnaswamy 1963, 250). One film, however, marks a turning point in the history of Hindi film circulation in Iran. It is the same film that Iranian film historian Javad Zeiny calls "the trigger of influence" (Zeiny 2015, 63): Raj Kapoor's *Sangam* (1964). The film was released in Iran at the same time as in India and remained in theaters for months, even years, drawing crowds of viewers to the point of selling a "million dollars' worth of tickets" (Zeiny 2015, 63).

Behind this success was a family of Hindu Sindhi merchants at the origin of the film's distribution in Iran: the Hinduja family. Even if Hinduja's cinematographic history begins with Raj Kapoor's film *Shree 420* (1955), it is *Sangam* (1964) that marks the breaking point. The family holds the

[1] Ardeshir Irani marked the history of Indian cinema by making the first Indian talking film in 1931, *Alam Ara*.

international distribution rights of the film, and thanks to this success, it entered the field of film distribution for good.

One of the characteristics of the Indian industry is that it is structured around individuals or families, as Baburao K. Pai noted:

> Our institutions are mostly individualistic, in almost all branches of the industry. If a person leaves the concern, or dies, the institution also dies with him. Such is not the case with the more organised western industry. Take for example, MGM.; both the Ms and G have left the concern, but still MGM. is running to the same standard and capacity. (Pai in Ray 2009, 199)

Film studios, such as Mehboob Khan's and Raj Kapoor's, whose films circulate internationally, do not follow the vertical integration model of Hollywood majors. To distribute their films abroad, they must rely on strong networks with international links. The Hinduja family has this capacity and takes advantage of a long trading relationship with Iran to start distributing in a country that already has a historic proximity to Indian film culture.

Originally from the Shikarpuri region, the Hinduja family established its first trading relationship with Iran. The most prominent merchant of the region, Srichand Hinduja, started his business in 1919, initially in textiles. Based in the town of Shikarpur in Sindh, he traded a variety of products in Iran: spices, fruits and vegetables, and cutlery. A few years later, he established his business here, the first outside of India, according to the Hinduja Group website. At the time of the Partition between India and Pakistan in 1947, the Hinduja family left the Sindh region, now in Pakistan, to settle in Bombay. Srichand Hinduja eventually made his fortune and invested largely in real estate, laying the foundation for one of the largest Indian trading companies of the twenty-first century, although the Hinduja family's business truly took off in the 1960s (Markovits 2000, 107). After the Iranian Revolution, the family moved the company's headquarters from Iran to London in 1979, from where it operates in a multitude of sectors: banking, finance, media, energy, health, and real estate. Founders of a now international empire,[2] the Hinduja family counts among it the richest men in the United Kingdom. At the head of the group is Srichand P. Hinduja, with his brothers Gopichand, Prakash, and

---

[2] Markovits notes the attention given today to Sindhis as "global tribes" and their role in our globalized world (Markovits 2000).

Ashok at his side. The role of this family in the film industry remains poorly understood and even obscure. On their website, in the media and entertainment section, they make a furtive mention:

> On the movie front INEL and its predecessor companies have been associated with the biggest Bollywood banners since the 1950s starting with international distribution rights of Raj Kapoor's blockbuster. More recently INEL financed the Amitabh Bachchan, Hema Malini family saga *Baghbaan* and Sonny Deol's *Bhagat Singh*. INEL provides a full range of services including funding, production, distribution and exhibition.[3]

If this official discourse confirms the relations between Raj Kapoor and the Hinduja, the modalities of these links and the exact role of the family in the distribution of the film has not been documented. From this slice of history of transnational circulation,—in the absence of being able to meet the family itself or to access the archives of the Kapoor house—the stories and anecdotes form sources of the first order. Mention of the Hinduja appears in a biography of Raj Kapoor written by his daughter, Ritu Nanda. In the chapter "Friends & Colleagues," along with other film personalities, the Hinduja are remembered:

> Paying tribute to Raj Kapoor, the Hindujas recall: 'In 1957 we started distributing his many masterpieces to world audiences. At the many premiers we organized overseas, fans became ecstatic! This business association transformed into a close family relationship between us and Raj, Krishnaji (the centre of his life) and his gifted children. This relationship with Raj Kapoor remains among our fondest memories'. (Nanda and Kapura 2002, 90)

This text accompanies a photo of the Hindujas with the Kapoor family, without mentioning the first names of each member of the Hinduja family. However, could this tribute be a watered-down version of the more ambiguous links between Raj Kapoor and the Hinduja family? An interview I conducted with Jaya Prakash (J. P.) Chowksey, Raj Kapoor's Madhya Pradesh-based distributor since the 1960s, outlines their relationship, and how they played a key role in disseminating Indian films to a Middle East that was not easily identifiable, between Iran, the Gulf, and

---

[3] Source: "Media & Entertainment," *Hinduja Group*, hindujagroup.com/global-investments/media-entertainment-30-11-2011/imcl.html, accessed July 29, 2016.

the rest of the region. His discourse also participates in the mysterious narrative around this family, since Hinduja designates, depending on the abstract family entity, a singular person or a set of people from the family.[4] Finally, beyond the singular and precise modalities of *Sangam*'s circulation in the Middle East, this interview reveals, on the one hand, the role of a merchant family from Sindh in cinematographic export. On the other hand, due to the impossibility of cross-checking this information with pre-existing detailed written sources, the interview testifies as well to the role that this family played in the imagination of Bombay's industrial circles. To better hear the story of the Hindujas, Raj Kapoor, and *Sangam*, as it may have circulated in the film world, I let J. P. Chowksey's words unfold.

> [For the shooting of *Sangam*] They went to a hill station near Bangalore. They shot a song and some scenes there. They came back ... Somebody told them, "It looks like it's shot in Europe!" So they said, "Let's go to Europe to shoot it!—But the script doesn't allow it!", "Who cares about the script! The couple is married, they're going on their honeymoon, so we're going to Europe, we're shooting there, in Paris and in England." During the honeymoon, there are two songs and many dramatic scenes. Raj Kapoor never made a film strictly following his script, he thought that a script evolved over time, that it kept changing. The shooting abroad was organized by the Hinduja. Hinduja is a very famous business company in London today. They are Indians, the Hinduja. At that time, Hinduja was a small trading company in Iran. Very small. However, one of the family members loved movies. Therefore, he went with Raj Kapoor to Europe to shoot and bought international rights. Then, Hinduja heard that the Shah of Iran had liked *Sangam*. He installed a projector in the Shah's palace, gave him a copy of the film and said, "Now you can watch it as many times as you like." The Shah liked the film so much that he gave commercial advantages to the Hinduja in importation/exportation in Iran. The distribution of *Sangam* created a business. The company of businessmen, Hinduja. They made money with *Sangam* and they truly developed their relationship with the Shah of Iran. And you know, to this day, the Hinduja are wanted by the Iranian police. They don't take a flight over Iran. Because they have made so much money with *Sangam*, their parent company is called Sangam International, its headquarters are in London. To complete the Hinduja story, they are a family of Sindhi merchants who are strictly vegetarian; they

---

[4] During the interview, I maintain these fluctuations, these uncertainties of language.

do not drink alcohol and follow the rules of the *dharm guru*.[5] So, having earned a lot of money from *Sangam*, they diversified their funds into various businesses and expanded. Meanwhile, Raj Kapoor took six years to finish *Mera Naam Joker*, which was ultimately a commercial failure, a huge bankruptcy. In those six years, the Hinduja empire had expanded everywhere. Now the Hinduja are coming back into Raj Kapoor's life. They say, "We owe you. You are making *Bobby*, a big budget film with big actors, we will finance your film". And the deal was to split the proceeds 50-50. Raj Kapoor had a big ego, and he didn't want to be paid less than 10 lakhs[6] for his film, the price a top actor demands. After the huge failure of *Joker* and another failure called *Kal Aaj Kal* directed by his son Randhir Kapoor, no one was willing to buy his film. Cinema is a cruel business. So Shashi Kapoor stepped in, he got the Delhi-UP circuit. Raj Kapoor said, "Okay, let's release the film in Delhi-UP. If the film does well, it will be distributed all over the world. And if it's a flop, it's a flop." The Hinduja went to file a complaint, because as long as Raj Kapoor had not paid back their 40 lakhs, how could he distribute the film?

These commercial dealings between the Hinduja and Kapoor families illustrate the financial system of the film industry, where production and distribution are inextricably linked. As Ganti explains, historically, one of the greatest difficulties for the Indian industry was raising funds to produce a film. Distributors, through the guaranteed minimum system, were a key source of funds. The guaranteed minimum allowed the director to finance the production of his film and granted the distributor theatrical rights. In this system, the distributors, who also played the role of producer, thus shared a large part of the financial risks of the film (Ganti 2012, 354).

So with international distribution and the Delhi and Punjab circuit, Raj Kapoor managed to get 22 lakhs. But he was still 18 lakhs short. At the time, Randhir Kapoor said that this film was a golden opportunity that the Hinduja did not understand. […] Since the Hinduja were not taking any risks, they had to give up their 50% shares. This allowed them to get their money back, so they accepted. The film turned out to be a huge success. It

---

[5] On their group's website, in the international trade section, it is mentioned: "*Today, the Hinduja Group trades internationally in practically all products and commodities except tobacco, meat and alcohol.*" Source: "International Trading—Trading and Merchandising," *Hinduja Group*, hindujagroup.com/international-trading/int.html, accessed July 29, 2016.

[6] That is one million Indian rupees, the equivalent of approximately 11,000 euros at the time of writing.

earned 1 crore[7] in the Punjab region alone. While the Hinduja bitterly regretted their decision, Raj Kapoor refused to see them again. He then made *Satyam Shivam Sundaram*, a commercial success but not very good artistically. After *Satyam Shivam Sundaram*, he directed *Prem Rog*. Before shooting, the Hinduja approached Randhir Kapoor and said, "We made a mistake, we want to apologize. As a token of our apology, please accept that we finance this film, without interest, without profit. Just return our investment without any interest and ask Raj Kapoor to forgive me." Randhir Kapoor convinced Raj Kapoor with these words, "Look, the funding system in India is poor. There are many difficulties, and the only practical solution is to accept. We could get other financing, but with interest. Here, we have financing, but without interest. And besides they apologize." He accepted because, in my opinion, he knew he was making a bold film, it dealt with widow remarriage in a feudal context, and the subject was delicate. He was aware of this, and he accepted this worthless financing. Hinduja's lawyer finally brought a copy of the agreement. Raj Kapoor's lawyer said that the agreement was good. But Raj Kapoor was very hurt by the Hinduja's behavior. So, he said, "I will sign this agreement, but not in my house. I will sign the agreement in their house. They know my rules, when I sign an agreement, I drink and I eat meat." They agreed. And they went into film distribution and into the Gulf with *Sangam*. After *Bobby*, the Hinduja financed many films with Amitabh Bachchan. Many films. When they financed Amitabh Bachchan's films, they also took international rights. You know, they were the champions of distribution for a long time, until the emergence of Eros International. At that time, there were two clans in the Hinduja family. One clan with the blessings of the Guruji and some members of the family had started drinking, so there was an internal dispute in the family. So they decided to stop the film business. They made a lot of money in the movie business. But never again with Raj Kapoor. After *Prem Rog*, he didn't want to work with them anymore, and fortunately, *Prem Rog* was a big success. Raj Kapoor was a man who was very vocal about his likes and dislikes. If he didn't like someone, he looked at them with deep contempt. And one could not believe that his eyes, which usually expressed love and kindness, could be so poisonous. So here is the story of the Hinduja in the distribution business.[8]

The history of the Hinduja and their involvement in the diffusion of Indian films in the region would not be complete without the story of the

---

[7] That is ten million Indian rupees, the equivalent of approximately 110,000 euros at the time of writing.
[8] Interview with J. P. Chowksey, December 4–5, 2014, in Indore.

Jumani family, with whom they share direct family ties. If the Hindujas take films from Bombay to Tehran, the Jumani family goes from Tehran to Beirut, before settling briefly in Cairo after the beginning of the Lebanese Civil War.

REFERENCES

Banda, Daniel, and José Moure, eds. 2008. *Le cinéma, naissance d'un art: premiers écrits (1895–1920)*. Champs. Paris: Flammarion.
Barnouw, Erik, and Subrahmanyam Krishnaswamy. 1963. *Indian Film*. New York; London: Columbia University Press.
Dutt, Guru, dir. 1957. *Pyaasa*.
———, dir. 1959. *Kaagaz ke Phool*.
Ganti, Tejaswini. 2012. *Producing Bollywood: Inside the Contemporary Hindi Film Industry*. Durham, NC: Duke University Press.
Garçon, François. 2006. *La distribution cinématographique en France (1907–1957)*. Paris: CNRS.
Grimaud, Emmanuel. 2003. *Bollywood Film Studio ou comment les films se font à Bombay*. Paris: CNRS éd.
Irani, Ardeshir, and Abdul Hossein Sepenta, dirs. 1932. *Dokhtare Lor Ya Irane Druz va Emruz*.
Kapoor, Raj, dir. 1949. *Barsaat*.
———, dir. 1951. *Awara*.
Khan, Mehboob, dir. 1949. *Andaz*.
———, dir. 1957. *Mother India*.
Markovits, Claude. 2000. *The Global World of Indian Merchants (1750–1947): Traders of Sind from Bukhara to Panama*. Cambridge Studies in Indian History and Society 6. Cambridge/New York: Cambridge University Press.
Nanda, Ritu, and Raja Kapura. 2002. *Raj Kapoor Speaks*. New Delhi/New York: Viking.
Nizami, Khaliq Ahmad. 1994. Early Arab Contact with South Asia. *Journal of Islamic Studies* 5 (1): 52–69.
Ray, R.M. 2009. *Indian Cinema in Retrospect*. New Delhi Gurgaon: Sangeet Natak Akademi Hope India Publications.
Thoraval, Yves. 2000. *Les cinémas du Moyen-Orient: Iran, Égypte, Turquie (1896–2000)*. Paris: Séguier.
Zeiny, Javad. 2015. *Le cinéma iranien: un cinéma national sous influences de 1900 à 1979 (avant la révolution)*. Paris: L'Harmattan.

CHAPTER 8

From Tehran to Beirut, the Jumani Brothers

Abstract This chapter offers a portrait of the Jumani family and its pivotal role in shaping the circulation of Indian cinema across the Middle East. Focused on the Jumani brothers' journey from Tehran to Beirut, the chapter unveils their important contribution to the transnational film trade.

In the 1960s, Iran emerged as a burgeoning cinema market, serving as a crucial meeting point for Indian distributors and their counterparts from Lebanon, Jordan, and Dubai. Recognizing the untapped potential of the Lebanese market, the Jumani brothers shifted their focus to Beirut, transforming it into a hub for the distribution of Hindi films in the Arab world. Their strategic subtitling choices underscored their profound understanding of regional dynamics, facilitating seamless exchanges with local film agents and adherence to linguistic preferences. By adapting subtitles to colloquial languages prevalent in each Middle Eastern territory, the Jumanis navigated complex linguistic landscapes, enhancing the accessibility and appeal of Indian films across the Middle East.

Keywords Indian Cinema • Beirut • Jumani Brothers • Subtitles • Transnational circulations • Portrait

We are the biggest supplier of Bollywood movies in the Middle East for over four decades. (Sanjay Jumani, Cannes, May 2018)

Difficult to locate in the written history of Indian cinema, the Jumani family is proportionally as discreet as their role has been important in the circulation of films in the Middle East. I discovered the first indication of the Jumani family's involvement in Lebanon in a book in Arabic on cinemas in Beirut, by the film critic, Mohammed Soueid:

> Before the incorporation of his company in 1952, before his sons took advantage of the Pigalle cinema, Indian films arrived in Lebanon through Indian distributors, such as the brothers Jumani & Ghour Mussan, and Nari Santani, and their Jordanian colleague Muhammad el-Thahir. With them, the number of Indian films arriving in Lebanon did not exceed one film per year.[1] (Soueid 1996, 72)

Based on this discovery, I started browsing through film archives and newspapers, looking for their name as distributors on films posters, yet the Jumani name was nowhere to be found.

Tehran: The Meeting Point

While reading a first draft of my manuscript, my supervisor, Catherine Servan-Schreiber asked me if it was possible to have more information on these Indian distributors. My readings and research, also dependent on an Arabic transcription of an Indian name, did not lead me to discover anything more. I had resigned myself to the fact that the Jumani brothers, and with them the names of Ghour Mussan and Nari Santani, remain obscure characters with blurred silhouettes, lurking in the shadow of history. Yet, in the summer of 2017, I made a surprising discovery when I was invited as a distributor to the Locarno Film Festival for its "Open Doors" section dedicated to young talents from South Asia. I met several Indian distributors at the festival. As I was presenting the topic of my research to one of them, he said: "But I lived in Beirut, I even speak a little Arabic, I used to travel there with my brother." Imagine my surprise, my interlocutor was none other than Sanjay Jumani, the younger brother of Ranchor Jumani, who established an office in Beirut in the late 1960s. Ranchor Jumani was initially based in Tehran, and worked jointly with his maternal uncles' family, the Hinduja branch. As Ranchor Jumani himself states, "Tehran was a stopover for filmmakers before they went to shoot

---

[1] I translate from Arabic.

elsewhere. Directors, like Shakti Samanta with *An Evening in Paris*, would first stop in Tehran to raise money for the film, and only then would they go to shoot in Beirut, for example."[2] In this configuration, Tehran constitutes an essential nodal point in the meetings with other distributors in the Arab space. The Jumani brothers met with Lebanese and Jordanian distributors, as well as with distributors from Dubai.

In the 1960s, Iran was a booming market for cinema, with a marked increase in the number of cinemas and attendance. It was in Tehran that Indian distributors met Lebanese distributors. Although Hollywood Majors had local offices in the Iranian capital until the 1970s, Iran was also part of the territories supervised by the regional offices based in Beirut. Lebanese distributors therefore went to Tehran to distribute their mandated American films. Ranchor Jumani discovered the potential of the Lebanese market, a territory that was still almost virgin to Indian films.

BEIRUT, STARTING POINT FOR NEW TRANSNATIONAL CIRCULATIONS

In Beirut, the Jumani brothers met distributors from other Arab countries. Leaving Tehran and opening an office in Beirut, a crucial city for the distribution of foreign films, the Jumani brothers organized a new geography for the circulation of Hindi films in the Arab space. "In Beirut, Sanjay Jumani tells me, we used to sell our films to the Jordanian 'brothers' Mohammad Taher and his cousin, Youssef Taher.[3] They were based in Jordan, they came to Bombay. In reality, we met in Tehran because the trips were usually made through Iran. There, the Taher brothers became friends with the family."[4] The Jordanian market "becomes a big market for Hindi films" with the 1970 war. Sanjay Jumani is most probably referring to the short-lived Civil War in Jordan, most commonly referred to as "Black September," which resulted in the exit of Palestine Liberation Organization (PLO) forces from Jordan to Lebanon. The Jordanian network appears again in Sanjay Jumani's speech at the time of the Lebanese Civil War: "During the war, Lebanese distributors would drive to Jordan to pick up the films. They used to get on buses that took them across the

[2] Interview with Ranchor Jumani, Cannes, May 14, 2018.
[3] Brothers or cousins, the relationship is not clear.
[4] Interview with Sanjay Jumani, Cannes, May 16, 2018.

border, it was not very far."⁵ The Jordanian distributors then made the link with the distribution of films in the Palestinian territories, until "the Palestinians," adds Sanjay Jumani, "started buying directly from us, without going through the Jordanians. There was this buyer on the Palestinian side of Jerusalem, Assad Freteak.⁶ And even in the 1970s, after the Sadat pact, we were printing copies with Hebrew subtitles."⁷

The heyday of Hindi films in Beirut reached its peak during the Jumani brothers' presence in Beirut in pre-war Lebanon. Ranchor Jumani had his office for about five years in the capital, before moving to Cairo, after the outbreak of the Civil War. In the Lebanese capital, he met the Indian distributor Gurmuk Singh, who has been established in the country for a few years. "Gurmuk Singh lived alone in Beirut," Ranchor Jumani tells me. "He loved my wife's cooking and so I often invited him to lunch at my place as he lived alone."⁸

SUBTITLES AS A GEOGRAPHIC DISTRIBUTION STRATEGY

The subtitling choices the Jumani brothers made to distribute their movies highlights their in-depth knowledge of the region, their interactions with other film agents, and the exchanges in good practices. The distribution network organization also operated according to the criterion of subtitles superimposed on the original copy. The Jumani brothers understood well this spatial organization and made their decisions according to the territories where they were going to broadcast their films. As the Indian Goodwill Trade Mission to the Middle East Countries in 1954 simply stated: "the Mission recommend that Indian films dubbed for export to the Middle East should be in the colloquial language current in Egypt" (Birla 1955, 11–12). The Jumani brothers managed to add the polyglot dimension in subtitles, based on their knowledge on the field, per country of the Middle East.

"In order to maximize the circulation of the copy in different countries, double subtitling was used for the most part. A copy with French and

---

⁵ Interview with Sanjay Jumani, Cannes, May 16, 2018.
⁶ Sanjay Jumani tells me the spelling of his name, which I'm using here, but which doesn't really correspond to the transcription of an Arabic name.
⁷ Interview with Sanjay Jumani, Cannes, May 16, 2018.
⁸ Interview with Ranchor Jumani, Cannes, May 14, 2018.

Arabic subtitles allowed for circulation in North Africa, and a copy with English subtitles circulated in the English-speaking areas of the region,"[9] testifies Sanjay Jumani. While the Lebanese laboratories were destroyed during the war, Ranchor Jumani left Beirut for Cairo, where he officially registered his company, to continue his activities. In the Egyptian capital, he met the Egyptian distributor Sobhi, to whom he sold some of his films. To subtitle their films, the Jumanis worked with one of the most renowned persons in subtitling in Egypt, Anis Obeid (1909–1988), who specialized in translating and subtitling foreign films in Arabic in Egypt. Historically, Arabic subtitling "originated in Egypt with the debut of Titra Film in 1932, followed in 1940 by Anis Obeid's subtitling company, which dominated the market for many years" (el-Khoury 2011, 81).

The Jumani brothers scoured several cities in the Arab world to distribute their films, from Tehran to Beirut, from Lebanon to Cairo, until they opened an office in Istanbul in the 1970s. The movement of these merchants simultaneously created a network of local distributors. The Jumani brothers appear to be one of the crucial links in this transnational circuit, that was also of influence in facilitating shooting of Bollywood movies in Beirut.

REFERENCES

Birla, M.P. 1955. *Report Indian Goodwill Trade Mission to the Middle East Countries (1954–1955)*. New Delhi: Government of India, Ministry of Commerce and Industry.

el-Khoury, Tatiana. 2011. Le sous-titrage dans le monde arabe : contraintes et créativité. In *Traduction et médias audiovisuels*, ed. Adriana Șerban and Jean-Marc Lavaur. Arts du spectacle. Villeneuve d'Ascq (France): Presses Universitaires du Septentrion.

Soueid, Mohammad. 1996. *Ya fu'adi: sirat sinamai'it ʿan salat Birut alrahla*. Beyrouth: Dar Al Nahar.

[9] Interview with Sanjay Jumani, Cannes, May 16, 2018.

CHAPTER 9

Bollywood Shoots Beirut, Beirut Screens Bollywood

Abstract During the 1960s, Beirut emerged as a vibrant hub for international film productions, contributing to Lebanon's cinematic attractivity. This chapter delves into the dynamic relationship between Bollywood and Beirut, exploring both film exhibition and production aspects. It demonstrates how Hindi films were part of marginalized distribution circuits while shaping perceptions of the Lebanese capital.

By analyzing the portrayal of Beirut in two iconic Bollywood movies, *An Evening in Paris* and *Ankhen*, this chapter unveils the city's dual image as a glamorous tourist destination and a center of international intrigue. *An Evening in Paris* showcases Beirut's coastal charm and leisure activities, while *Ankhen* transforms it into a backdrop for espionage narratives. This aesthetic underscores Bollywood's resonance with the international imagery of Beirut and Bollywood's alignment with Beirut's global perception.

Keywords Beirut • Espionage • Spy Films • Tourism • *Ankhen* • Film shooting

The 1960s marked a Golden Age for the Beirut film industry. The city attracted international film productions, and Lebanese cinema benefited from the arrival of Egyptian talents, fleeing the country since the nationalization of Egyptian cinema in 1963. The production, distribution, and exhibition sectors thrived: Lebanon produced 20 films in 1967 and, despite this low number, ranked second among Arab countries. The attendance index in cinemas in 1961 was four times higher than in France and ten times higher than in Egypt. Shooting Hindi films in Beirut was favored by the local settlement of the Jumani brothers in the Lebanese capital. They contribute to forge new transnational links between India and the Middle East as well as have Bollywood in tune with the international imagery of Beirut.

BOLLYWOOD IN THE MARGINS: THE DISTRIBUTION AND EXHIBITION INDUSTRIES IN BEIRUT

Beirut was on the map as a center for film distribution, as the Hollywood majors had the Lebanese capital as their headquarters for distribution in the region. The pre-eminence of commercial networks in the circulation of films in Lebanon can be explained in particular by the liberal commercial policy for the import of films into the country, already in the 1960s: "The Lebanese government imposes no restrictions on the import of films into the national territory; the import is 'controlled' by means of a customs duty set at 50 Lebanese pounds per kilogram of imported film" (Monaco 1966, 143). Structurally, the arrival of foreign films in the country is not under the tutelage of a state agency. The presence and distribution of films are based on private initiatives, with no State incentive to preserve national cinema or favor Arab films in general. Less studied than the circulation of Hollywood films in the region,[1] Indian films in Lebanon still have left their mark in written sources and through film posters (Fig. 9.1). Mohammed Soueid, a film critic, gives some details about the presence of Indian films on Beirut screens.

The first success of an Indian film in Lebanon to which Soueid refers in his book, although the archives of the French language national daily

---

[1] See the works of Melnick, Ross. *Hollywood's Embassies: How Movie Theaters Projected American Power around the World*. Film and Culture. New York [New York]: Columbia University Press, 2022. Mingant, Nolwenn. *Hollywood Films in North Africa and the Middle East: A History of Circulation*. SUNY Series, Horizons of Cinema. Albany: State University of New York Press, 2022.

Fig. 9.1 Indian Movie Posters from the Collection of 'Aboudi Bou Jawdah. (Source: Personal archives, photos taken in June 2014 in Beirut)

L'Orient-Le-Jour attest to the programming of the film *Sangam* (Kapoor 1964) at the Cinema Rivoli for five consecutive weeks in 1965, was not that of a film by Raj Kapoor but that of Shakti Samanta:

> In 1967, following the unexpected success of the Hindi film *Al-'Ibadah* [original title: *Aradhana*] with Sharmila Tagore as the heroine, and Shakti Samanta as the director, the Pigalle became the only venue intended for the screening of the sung and maudlin melodramas imported from Indian studios. Distributor Zouheir el-Sabban, one of Mohammad Khalid el-Sabban's sons, traces Indian production in Lebanon back to before the Pigalle cinema. It is true that his late father was at the origin of the distribution of Indian melodrama, but his role was first to organize the programming of Indian films. (Soueid 1996, 72)

The Pigalle cinema was established in Dabbas Square. The history of the existence of this cinema "remains full of mysteries," in the words of Soueid. According to his information, it was said to have been created by a Jew of Iraqi origin named Youssef Khadra. The official story, the one that everyone knows, is that this cinema appeared in 1964. Cinemas were usually built on the remains of garages or inns. The Pigalle, on the contrary, was built on the place of an ice cream factory that, due to the repeated bankruptcies of its owner, Moustafa Mousalli, was sold in 1966 to the company of Mohammad Khalid el-Sabban & sons (Fig. 9.2).

In the center of Beirut, two streets compete in terms of movie theaters: Bliss Street and Hamra Street. Between the two competing streets, a new cinema, Le Baron, appeared in the early 1960s not far from al-Khalidi hospital, and close to the Edison cinema. This cinema was established by a Syrian, Adnan Deir Atani, who was able to amass a fortune amounting to several millions for investing in the Indian film *Ibnu-l-ḥarām*, which he previewed at the Rivoli big screen, where *Sangam* was also screened. This film would correspond to Mehboob Khan's *Son of India*, released in India in 1962.

With the arrival of the Sabban family, Indian productions piled up on the screens of the Pigalle cinema in Beirut, and it began to welcome an audience, most of whom were from both the Indian and Pakistani communities. In addition to this community audience, Armenians made up about 70% of the audience at Saturday screenings, writes Mohammed

Fig. 9.2 *Junglee* (Subodh Mukherji 1961) at Cinema Pigalle (Beirut). (Source: Excerpt from Antoine Kabbabé personal video archives dating back to 1973, Cinema Pigalle (Beirut))

Soueid.[2] The author continues by comparing the strategy of the Pigalle to that of the Alphonse cinema, which was mainly aimed at an audience from the French community, while the Pigalle distinguished itself "by attracting an audience of minorities and the category of migrant workers, working and residing on Lebanese territory". He adds,

> The spread of the Indian melodrama to different theaters in the depths of the al-Burj district[3] has shed light on these theaters that cater to the popular and general taste, and to the pleasure of social classes outside the elite. These social classes have found in the melodrama a show where their daily misery and poverty are projected. (Soueid 1996, 72)

The analysis of audiences in terms of minority communities or foreign migrant workers echoes the strategy of exoticization of audiences that is

---

[2] Based on an interview conducted by Mohammed Soueid with Zouheir el-Sabban and published in the newspaper *Al-safir* on April 25, 1983 (as a note in Soueid's book).
[3] To expand on the Armenian community in Lebanon and their relationship to Indian films, see Sunya, Samhita. "On Location: Tracking Secret Agents and Films, between Bombay and Beirut." *Film History: An International Journal* 32, no. 3 (2020): 105–40.

also found in the Greek case in relation to Indian films, as highlighted in the article, *A Cultural Colony of India* (Eleftheriotis 2006). However, Eleftheriotis points out that this is an exoticization of Greek spectators, drawing on the work of Abadzi and Tasoulas, who themselves offer examples of this elitism by denigrating these spectators with terms such as: little people, *"tsemperia"* (veiled), a term used to describe "poor women," using Orientalist referents. For Eleftheriotis, their work, dominated by the desire to collect data, participates in the division of audiences into two categories: the middle-class who perceive Indian cinema with the necessary distance of irony, and the working-class, victim of an ideological misidentification. In this rhetoric, Indian film remains profoundly Other, either as an exotic product of another culture or as a source of low entertainment for an "other" audience (Eleftheriotis 2006, 109). In the same way, in the Lebanese case, this cinema is perceived as a popular entertainment, practiced by populations in the margins, "other," first identified by their community origins (Indian, Pakistani, Armenian) and by their social class. The analysis echoes that offered by the French historian at the UNESCO conference "Cinema and Arab culture" in 1965. According to the report, "Mr. Sadoul then shows how the Arab popular class has ensured the success of Indian films. He wonders if the Indian film does not constitute for this social stratum a diversion from its daily reality" (Centre interarabe du cinéma et de la télévision 1965). The observations of Soueid and Sadoul are in contradiction, since one sees an identification of popular audiences with the images on the screen, while the other perceives it on the contrary as a form of escapism.

In the absence of proper audience studies in the cinemas of Lebanon in the 1960s, we can only infer how Indian films were perceived in relation to their audiences. Indian cinema seems to be confined to an exoticism acceptable for a non-Lebanese public, where elitist contempt joined a compartmentalization of society, operating a division between the Lebanese and the Others. Hindi cinema in Lebanon, as in the Egyptian case, functions as a social marker. If the first great Indian successes managed to be taken up by first-class cinemas, for an audience of "good taste," their displacement in time and space gradually pushed Indian films to the side of the circuits of the cinema business, alongside karate, kung-fu films, or spaghetti westerns.

1967, *An Evening in Paris*: Beirut as a Stop-Over, Shooting on the Way to Europe

The sequence shot abroad is an essential symbol of Bollywood films in the collective imagination and appears as a constitutive motif of the Bollywood style. It really took off in the 1960s, as the frenzy of color took hold of Bollywood's filmmakers and fueled their desire to travel and to shoot on natural sets. The development of new cameras and new cinematographic techniques contributed to the transformation of the representation of places and geographical spaces in Hindi cinema. The arrival of lighter cameras, better equipped for outdoor sound recording, and the deployment of color favored outdoor filming, used mostly for romantic sequences and their inevitable accompaniment, songs. The development of Eastmancolor technology in India in the early 1960s facilitated this process. Previously, Technicolor's three-film trichromatic process required intense lighting on set, and Technicolor required a color supervisor or color consultant on every shoot. Second, the imbibition print was complex, requiring the three trichrome selection negatives to be printed separately before the three strips could be merged (Mannoni 2016, 154). As a result, studios in India had to send Technicolor films back to the US lab for printing. By contrast, the Eastman monopack was simpler to use and required only one film to be shot, although it was criticized for less stable colors over time. Nonetheless, this enabled Hindi cinema to tame its own exotic world in color: essentially the Western world, with the first shootings abroad in Europe.

Films like *Junglee* (Subodh Mukherji, 1960), *Kashmir Ki Kali* (Shakti Samanta, 1963), *Sangam* (Raj Kapoor, 1964), and *An Evening in Paris* (Shakti Samanta 1967) set the visual and narrative convention for using exterior settings. They functioned as animated postcards and presented tourist sites to the viewer at a time when a whole imaginary of the Indian middle class was being condensed around travel (Mazumdar 2011). At the same time, the development of airplanes made them a means of transportation accessible to a larger segment of the population and favored the development of tourism. In this sense, these sequences take up, in their style, aspects of the tourist film: to present the iconic places and monuments of the country, to create dream images, and to incite to travel. They are like small tourist films within the great cinematographic narrative.

The deployment of air routes in the 1960s favored India's connection with Europe, via the Middle East, a necessary stopover point. Air India offered routes linking Bombay to the Arabian Peninsula as well as to Beirut and Cairo.[4] The 1960s also coincided with the advent of Beirut as a center of air traffic in the route between East and West. The Lebanese capital was a central stopover point for long-haul flights to Europe, providing an easily accessible stopover on the way to Europe.

Building on its centrality between the East and the West and its touristic appeal as the "Paris of the Middle East" or the "Switzerland of the Middle East," Beirut sought to attract more tourists and film shootings. This strategy appeared in the Egyptian press, for instance, where Lebanon was described as "land of milk and honey" or "land of hospitality. Unique landscapes. Emerald sea. Majestic mountains."[5] The same arguments are presented in Sadoul's book *Les cinémas des pays arabes* (1966). Lucienne Khoury, in her chapter on the prospects of Lebanese cinema, insists on the beauty and variety of the country's landscapes to attract foreign filming:

> Moreover, the variety of landscapes, rocky or wooded mountains, green or desert plains, steep or sandy coasts, the ideal climate which allows to guarantee good weather during long periods, the flowering of luxurious hotels and modern beaches, finally a cheap labor force and extras make it possible to carry out films under pleasant, fast and economic conditions and, thus, can attract foreign capital and bring producers to carry out films in Lebanon. (Khoury 1966, 229)

The first Hindi film shot in Beirut, *An Evening in Paris* (Samanta 1967), features the city as a resort. It is a stopover during the amorous chase between our two protagonists since, seeking to escape from Sam, her suitor, Deepa goes to Switzerland and then to Beirut.[6] The viewer learns that Deepa is in Beirut through the conversation of a gang of criminals trying to locate her, in order to kidnap her and ask for a ransom from her millionaire father. From the place of the cabaret, the spectator switches to a shot of the sea to the sounds of a music that evokes carefreeness, and we find Deepa and her maid, Honey, lying in a deckchair and sipping a Coca-Cola. In search of strong sensations to forget Sam, Deepa absolutely

---

[4] A brief history of Air India's routes to the Middle East shows that the routes follow the political tensions in the region. They also indicate the growing importance of the Gulf countries as they gradually appear on the airline's route map and the increase in scheduled flights (Smith 2002, 229–39).

[5] In, respectively, *Le Journal d'Égypte*, April 3, 1968 and June 22, 1968.

[6] Clearly, the narrative serves as a pretext for traveling to as many cities as possible. In each city, Sam finds Deepa and employs various strategies to seduce her.

wants to make a tour on a jet-ski. Between the sea, the pool, and the jet-ski, all the elements of the tourist film are there, while evoking a Lebanese *art de vivre*.
The imagination of the Lebanese capital is embodied by its coast, its seaside, and its famous pigeon cave. Beirut evokes the luxury of a seaside life, its private swimming pools, and its maritime leisure activities, such as boating or jet-skiing. The Beirut sequence of the film is typical of the tourist films made by companies like British Pathé or MovieTone. British Pathé's *Holidays in Beirut* (1971), with its images of people sitting by a pool, carefree, echoes the Beirut sequence in *An Evening in Paris*. However, unlike the tourist films that highlight the cultural and historical heritage of the country (Baalbeck, the caves of Jeita), the scenes of traditional life (fishermen by the water), Lebanese gastronomy (mezzes), and the capital of the country as a financial center (presence of many banks), this Bollywood film does not insist on local singularities. The ambition is mainly to film its characters in a dreamy setting, and to set up spectacular scenes such as Shammi Kapoor helicopter scene, chasing his girlfriend on his jet-ski[7] (Sunya 2020, 116).

1968, *ANKHEN*: BEIRUT, CITY OF SPIES

In the category of the spy film, the reference to Lebanon unites the American, European, and Indian cinematographic imaginations. Not in the staging of the shootings in natural settings but rather in the evocation of the city as a center of international espionage. The Lebanese director Jocelyne Saab presents the argument in her film *Once Upon A Time: Beirut, the History of a Star* (1994), a film-montage that uses sequences from American and European films shot in Lebanon. In a poetic and argumentative fable, the images display Lebanon as a frequent backdrop for spy films. From *La Châtelaine du Liban* (Pottier 1956) to *Le spie uccidono a Beirut* (Martino and Loy 1965), Beirut embodies the city of espionage. The cinematographic golden age of Lebanon in the 1960s saw many foreign films shot on its soil, among which we can cite the most emblematic: *Échappement libre* (Becker 1964), *Where the Spies Are* (Guest 1965), *La Grande sauterelle* (Lautner 1967), or *Embassy* (Hessler 1972). In addition, "other B movies are also shot in Lebanon: Beirut being presented in these films as a center of conspiracy, espionage, trafficking" (Zaccak 1997,

---

[7] The helicopter, with the insignia of the Lebanese flag, must belong to the Lebanese army and testifies to the assistance of the country's army in the shooting of the film.

48). This imaginary is already present in literature, since *La Châtelaine du Liban* and *Embassy* are both films adapted from novels of the same name. While Lebanese technicians and actors supervise the foreign teams, this imaginary penetrates even the Arab productions themselves. An Egyptian film, co-produced with Syria, such as *Meeting in Palmyra* (Original title, *Liqaa fi tudamir*, Maalouf 1965), "is an adventure film that takes place between Beirut, Baalbeck and Palmyra, and as always the plot of the malefactors is prepared in Beirut, 'the center of international plots'" (Zaccak 1997, 88). Each of these films conforms to the expected motifs of the spy film, with its share of cabaret and oriental dance scenes in the style of Mata Hari, spectacular chases in the city, and airport scenes.

At the same time, testifying to a convergence and circulation of the imaginary, Bollywood tried its hand at the genre of the spy film for the first time with *Ankhen* by Ramanand Sagar (1968). Considered the pioneer of the genre in Hindi cinema, it takes up the typical motifs of the spy film, intertwining politics, adventures, and travel to various exotic locations in the manner of James Bond films (Cinémathèque française 2023). While the Cold War is the political background of many American spy films, *Ankhen* shows another geopolitical concern: that of a democracy in danger under the terrorist attacks of an internal enemy. In *Ankhen,* the Middle East serves as a relocated space to evoke the struggle with its enemy brother, Pakistan. In this respect, the film features a typical backdrop of paranoia about the aggression of a country "that wants to destroy Indian democracy" (dialogue from the movie), without the name of the latter ever being mentioned. However, the viewer guesses that it is Pakistan since the opening scene evokes attempts to destabilize India through terrorist attacks in Assam.

Ankhen, working at the junction between the travel film and the spy film, takes us from India to Japan via Beirut, the meeting point of international espionage (Sunya 2020, 129). In this film, through the choice of locations in the country, the direction seeks above all a form of monumentality: we film spectacular and recognizable places, such as the Cave of Pigeons in a mythical scene of maritime chase, or the temple of Baalbeck and its masterful columns, or the citadel of Jbeil. All these places are the many tourist tropes of the country that serve as spectacular backdrops to create great scenes of suspense and action. The heyday of filming on Lebanese soil ended with the beginning of the Civil War. For almost 40 years, no Hindi film set foot on Lebanese soil again. Ironically, Lebanon's conflicted history is what allows the country to land war films today and to offer battle scenes in natural settings that are more than realistic. The remnants of the country's ruins and the possibility of staging an explosion in the streets of Beirut were the commercial arguments to attract the shooting of Kabir Khan's film in the nets of the Lebanese capital. Only the impossibility of shooting these scenes in Dubai led Indian director Kabir Khan to shoot in Lebanon in 2014 for his spy film, *Phantom*.

This anecdote shows how differently the ecosystem for Indian films has grown in the Middle East. As Dubai has become a central node for Indian film production and distribution in the mid-2000s, part IV dwells on understanding the shifts that operated in the decades 1970s to 2000s, be it shifts in localities, in audiences, or in screening spaces.

REFERENCES

Becker, Jean, dir. 1964. *Échappement Libre*.
Centre interarabe du cinéma et de la télévision. 1965. *Cinéma et Cultures Arabes. IVème Conférence de La Table Ronde Organisée Avec l'aide Technique de l'UNESCO*. Liban: Beyrouth.
Cinémathèque française. 2023. *Top Secret—Cinéma & Espionnage*. Flammarion. Paris.
Eleftheriotis, Dimitris. 2006. A Cultural Colony of India. *South Asian Popular Culture* 4 (2): 101–112.
Guest, Val, dir. 1965. *Where the Spies Are*.
Hessler, Gordon, dir. 1972. *Embassy*.
Kapoor, Raj, dir. 1964. *Sangam*.
Khoury, Lucienne. 1966. Perspectives Du Cinéma Libanais. In *Les Cinémas Des Pays Arabes*, ed. Georges Sadoul, 228–233. Beyrouth: Centre Interarabe du Cinéma et de la Télévision.
Lautner, Georges, dir. 1967. *La Grande Sauterelle*.
Maalouf, Youssef, dir. 1965. *Liqaa Fi Tudamir*.
Mannoni, Laurent. 2016. La machine cinéma: de Méliès à la 3D [exposition, Paris, Cinémathèque française, 5 octobre 2016–29 janvier 2017]. Edited by Cinémathèque française. Paris: Cinémathèque française.
Martino, Luciano, and Mino Loy, dirs. 1965. *Le Spie Uccidono a Beirut*.
Mazumdar, Ranjani. 2011. Aviation, Tourism and Dreaming in 1960s Bombay Cinema. *BioScope: South Asian Screen Studies* 2 (2): 129–155.
Monaco, Eitel. 1966. Exploitation, Distribution, Importation Des Films. In *Les Cinémas Des Pays Arabes*, ed. Georges Sadoul, 164–165. Beyrouth: Centre Interarabe du Cinéma et de la Télévision.

Pottier, Richard, dir. 1956. *La Châtelaine Du Liban.*
Samanta, Shakti, dir. 1967. *An Evening in Paris.*
Smith, Myron Jack. 2002. *The Airline Encyclopedia (1909–2000).* 3 vols. Lanham, MD: Scarecrow Press.
Soueid, Mohammad. 1996. *Ya fu'adi: sirat sinamai'it ʿan salat Birut alrahla.* Beyrouth: Dar Al Nahar.
Sunya, Samhita. 2020. On Location: Tracking Secret Agents and Films, between Bombay and Beirut. *Film History: An International Journal* 32 (3): 105–140.
Zaccak, Hady. 1997. *Le cinéma libanais: itinéraire d'un cinéma vers l'inconnu (1929–1996).* Beyrouth: Dar el-Machreq.

PART IV

1973–2007. Shifting Spaces, Shifting Audiences: Bollywood's Decades of Transition in the Arab World

CHAPTER 10

Shubra Palace's Hero: Badi' Sobhi, The Distributor That Created Bollywood's Golden Age

Abstract This chapter explores the transformative role of Badi' Sobhi, an Egyptian distributor, in shaping Bollywood's Golden Age in Egypt during the late twentieth century. Despite governmental restrictions on Hindi films post-1970, Sobhi navigated legal obstacles to satisfy the growing demand for Indian films.

Amidst geopolitical shifts and state policies aimed at safeguarding the national film industry, Sobhi strategically circumvented regulations, establishing a robust distribution network across Cairo and Alexandria. His efforts culminated in creating a thriving market for Bollywood films in Egypt, particularly in the Shubra district.

However, Sobhi's success faced challenges in the 2000s, including escalating film prices and changing audience preferences influenced by the emergence of multiplexes and Hollywood blockbusters. Despite Sobhi's efforts, the once-thriving era of Bollywood in Egypt gradually waned, reflecting broader societal transformations and urban developments.

Keywords Shubra Palace • Badi' Sobhi • State Policy • Egypt • Bollywood • Golden Age

"West Asia has become a major export market for Indian films after the break of Arab-Israeli hostilities. As far as film industry is concerned, at least

© The Author(s), under exclusive license to Springer Nature Switzerland AG 2024
N. Srour, *Bollywood Film Traffic*, Palgrave Studies in Arab Cinema, https://doi.org/10.1007/978-3-031-64491-7_10

the step taken by the Government of India to uphold the cause of Arabs has become a boon to the industry,"[1] noted the Indian *Film Trade* journal in 1975. After the Six Day War, two Indian movies hit "the movie theatres of the capital like rockets, *Sangam* (Kapoor 1964) and *Suraj* (Rao 1966)" (Shafik in Eleftheriotis and Iordanova 2006). As this chapter shows, it did not take long for the Egyptian government to fight back this foreign popularity. Though, paradoxically, the restrictive state policy against Hindi films did not prevent their massive, yet located, success.

1973, STATE FIGHT: DOWN WITH "KARATE FILMS," DOWN WITH INDIAN FILMS!

The fight against Hindi films in Egypt after 1970 is to be understood within the more global framework of a shift in Indo-Egypt foreign relations, and a state policy to protect the national film industry. The study devoted to the Cinemas of Arab Countries in 1966 highlights Egypt's quota policy:

> In the UAR, a 'screen quota' is in force on the basis of one week reserved for the screening of national production films out of four weeks of shows. This 'quota' and the increase in national production combined to determine a significant decline in imports of foreign films: from 431 films imported in 1955 to 294 in 1958. Almost all the imports were American (and English) films: 245 in 1958, compared to 19 Italian, 15 Russian (the Soviet Union had made a notable effort to penetrate the Arab world with some positive results) and 15 of other nationalities. (Monaco 1966, 141)

This protectionism allowed Egyptian movies to secure a reserved place on the screens of the country and to face the threat of an external hegemony, be it Hollywood, French, Italian, or Indian. However, if the volume of Indian films distributed in Egypt is a result of government measures regarding foreign films in general, the fact remains that Hindi films were specifically targeted by the Egyptian law, along with Hong Kong films.

Legal enforcement of reducing the presence of Hindi films was linked to a growing political distance between Egypt and India. While Nasser and Nehru had a strong relationship building the Non-Aligned movement,

---

[1] *Film Trade*, July 26, 1975.

Egypt and India foreign relations changed with Sadat's coming to power after Nasser's death on September 28, 1970.

> The reasons for this are partly historical and partly economic. India's past relations with Egypt have been the result of two complementary factors. First, the personal equation between Nehru and Nasser was important. No less important was India's hope of outflanking Pakistan's diplomacy in the Arab world by cultivating Egyptian friendship. But now, with both Nasser and Nehru dead and with Pakistan vanquished, the same considerations no longer apply. (Bhatia 1977)

During the Cold War, their relations grew distant as they "were on the opposite side of the ideological fence—Egypt moved closer to the U.S. and India bonded ever more closely with the Soviet Union" (Aneja 2012).

On the other hand, on the national level, the Egyptian film industry was paying the price of nationalization enforced in 1963, leading to a drastic drop in production combined with a reduction in the number of cinemas, whose condition gradually deteriorated as the state was lacking money to renovate them. Thus, between 1965 and 1969, the country imported between 80 and 89.7% of foreign films, while during the same period, local production in cinemas fluctuated between 10.3 and 15% in 1965 and 1966, respectively (UNESCO 1981, 18). During the same (1965–1969) period, the United States remained the main source of film supply, ranging from 46% at the low point of imports in 1969 to 71% at its peak in 1971, while Indian films enjoyed a ratio of 2.5%.

From the 1970s onwards, a committee, established on June 5, 1971, under the chairmanship of the directors' office of the Egyptian General Organization for Cinema, oversaw the issuing of import/export permits. The law limits the import of foreign films to a maximum of 300 per year. It also establishes a link of dependence between local production and the import of foreign films as each producer of an Arabic-language film is allowed to import three foreign films, a rule that applies to private sector producers as well. Depending on the nation, preferential regimes have been established. Some foreign organizations have been exempted from this rule. Among them, we can mention two convincing cases, falling under two different typologies, as defined in the Egyptian legislative texts. One is the case of a foreign distribution office set up in Egypt and controlled by the government or the public sector of the country in question, such as the Soviet state film export organization based in Cairo and authorized to import Russian films into Egypt. Second is the case of the offices of foreign companies from capitalist countries, such as the local branches of American firms, authorized to import films from their production house, films they have co-produced or for which they have helped with distribution, and films for which they hold exclusive distribution rights.

In 1970, 25 Indian films were released on Egyptian screens, a peak never reached before, according to available sources. In addition, the programming of films was continuous throughout the year, and many of them were shown simultaneously in different theaters, a configuration that was also unheard of. After this exponential distribution of Hindi films in Egyptian cinema halls after the Six Day War, Hindi films underwent a form of organized censorship.

In 1973–1974, the Egyptian government deployed several measures with the general aim of protecting the Egyptian film industry by controlling the presence of Indian and "karate" films (essentially Hong Kong films). Official Decree No. 181 of 1973 stipulated that any import of films from India or Hong Kong into Egypt required the reciprocal export of Egyptian films to those two countries. Films from India and Hong Kong could only be released in an Egyptian cinema if the office of cinema, theater, and music had received a confirmation slip from a bank stating that the Egyptian distributor had received, as a minimum, the sums of £2,000 for an Egyptian film exported to Hong Kong or £5,000 for an Egyptian film exported to India. This strict reciprocity requirement was only for Asian productions and was not required for European or American productions. The measures concerning the latter were more flexible, and simply required cinemas to give preference to Egyptian films when possible, and to reserve Muslim holidays for domestic productions only. In terms of volume, the importation of "karate films" and Indian films was limited to 5 per year. The conditions of screening were also to be strictly controlled, as "the dates, conditions and rates of screening of these films must be approved by the General Organization for Cinema, Theatre and Music, and the organization will determine which cinemas will screen these films" (UNESCO 1981, 23).

The decrees issued in 1973 were aimed at protecting and promoting local production, against karate and Indian films, and not against American or European productions, which did not endanger Arabic-language film in the same way: "Egyptian cinema began to feel a serious lack of capital precisely when Indian films became a threat to the markets in which the local product was most effectively marketed" (Armbrust 2008, 211). A few measures forced the presence of the local film on the screens: as long as an Egyptian film brought in a minimum amount of revenue, the cinema was forbidden to stop programming it; all cinemas in Egypt had to show local films on the occasion of the two major Muslim holidays, Eid al-Adha and Eid al-Fitr, and Egyptian films had always to be given priority. As for the decree of March 10, 1973, it prohibited the screening of more than one "karate film" and more than one Indian film simultaneously and limited the screening to a maximum of five weeks, regardless of the films' revenues.

A decree of May 7, 1973, specified the programming of three public sector cinemas: previously reserved for Arabic-language films, these cinemas were now authorized by the Ministry of Culture and Information to show foreign films in the months of May and June, but also more than one Indian and "karate film" at a time, only in May and June. These measures posed important obstacles to the distribution of Indian films, yet Egyptian distributor Badi' Sobhi found a way around the law in order to match popular demand for Hindi films.

1985–1991: BOLLYWOOD'S GOLDEN AGE IN SHUBRA

In first-class cinemas, only a few Indian films circulated sporadically in the 1970s, until Badi' Sobhi, "the major importer of Indian films" took over this circuit (Iordanova 2006, 133). Owning cinema halls in both Cairo and Alexandria, he was able to create a distribution network in the most prominent cities in Egypt. Badi' Sobhi is the figure who embodies a transformation in film popular culture and was able to create a "golden" space for Bollywood films in Egypt by circumventing the laws that limited Hindi films' presence on cinema screens.

The Indian film distribution circuit in the 1980s was drastically transformed, both in the geography of the city's cinemas and in its audience. The first Hindi films, subtitled in French for the audience of foreign residents of downtown Cairo, were shown on the screens of an outlying district, Shubra. The countryside of Shubra developed and became urbanized in the nineteenth century, following the construction of the palace of Prince Mohamed Ali Tewfik. It was connected to Cairo by a beautiful 6 km long shaded alley leading to the ruler's estate, which made it a sought-after promenade. Today, Shubra is a popular and densely populated neighborhood of Cairo (Bénard 2016, 38, note 2). The first-class cinemas that had made a specialty of Indian film refused, in the late 1980s and early 1990s, to screen them again. The regular distribution of Hindi films in cinemas, with the exception of the Karim cinema in the city center, was then confined to second-class cinemas, such as the Cinema Modern or the famous Shubra Palace, owned by Badiʿ Sobhi himself, located in the neighborhood of the same name. The popular craze for Bollywood movies in second- and third-class cinemas is difficult to trace and measure through the local French- and English-speaking press. For this period, I will rely on the archives of the Arab press, the daily *Al-Ahram*, and on the testimony of Hourriya ʿAbdin who worked with Badiʿ Sobhi for over twenty years.[2]

The success, intense and dazzling, is condensed in a short period, from 1985 to 1991, considered as the golden age of Hindi cinema in Egypt as Hourriya ʿAbdin notes. I met ʿAbdin in May 2014 during my research fieldwork in Cairo; she worked in the distribution office of Badiʿ Sobhi as the head of commercial distribution of films from 1981 to around 2001. As sales manager, she was required to sell other Egyptian films in foreign territories, such as Morocco, since Sobhi distributed Egyptian films before specializing in Indian films. What was then described as the golden age of Hindi cinema was in fact very limited in time—only five years—and geographical space, as the films were essentially screened in two cinemas dedicated to Indian films: the Rialto cinema and Shubra Palace. This also placed limits on the social class of the audience, since these cinemas were situated in working-class neighborhoods, attracting a population of workers and students. Finally, this period was also limited in number—only about ten films were distributed by Sobhi. Before focusing on the distribution of Indian films, his cinema showed Indian titles such as *Sharaabi* (Mehra 1984) with the imposing Amitabh Bachchan. In its advertising communication, the Alexandria cinema, which also belongs to it, insists on programming *Coolie* (Desai and Raj 1983) "by popular demand,"[3] while the film breaks all records at the Shubra Palace cinema in Cairo, staying 15 weeks.[4]

Sobhi always used a specific business model. He began by distributing seven to eight films on which he would make no profit, but no loss either, the goal being to simply break even by reimbursing himself for the cost of transporting the print, the film rights, and advertising expenses from the

---

[2] Badiʿ Sobhi passed away at the age of 86, in 2006.
[3] *Al Ahram*, December 9, 1985, p. 12.
[4] *Al Ahram*, March 18, 1985, p. 12.

revenues. The film that ensured the success of his new venture was *Mard* (Desai 1985). Directed by Manmohan Desai, author of many successful films including *Amar, Akbar, Anthony* (Desai 1977b), *Dharam Veer* (Desai 1977a), or *Coolie* (Desai and Raj 1983). The film recounts the heroic struggle of a child of the people (Amitabh Bachchan)—who turns out to be the son of a prince—against the British oppressor. Egyptian audiences were already familiar with Manmohan Desai's films, as the abovementioned titles had been released in Egypt. The biggest commercial success of 1985 at the Indian box office, it was successful in Cairo as well, where it was released the following year, in 1986. As ʿAbdin explains, this film caused "a revolution in the Egyptian market": the story was beautiful, it featured

> a war against the English, and it was the same story in Egypt. And the fight against the English and the colonization were the foundations of the Egyptian people. In addition, the hero was very beautiful, the heroine very beautiful. […] It was the time of kung-fu and fighting movies. Those who wanted to see fight scenes were served, those who wanted to see beautiful landscapes and songs were served, those who wanted to see a story that resembled their own, they entered the theater and saw it on the screen.[5]

To promote the film, Badiʿ Sobhi conducted a major advertising campaign across both television and newspapers, relying on a trailer composed of eye-catching clips and a realistic, almost photographic style poster. It cost a whopping 250,000 Egyptian guineas, but the film was a phenomenal success in theaters, running for more than seven months. "With a ticket price of 20 or 30 piasters, the cinema that showed the film earned 4,000 to 6,000 Egyptian guineas a day!", ʿAbdin recalls.

At the same time, Egyptian actor Adil Imam's latest film was being released on Egyptian screens, but the failure was bitter against Amitabh Bachchan. War was then declared against the Hindi film, accused of endangering local film production, draining the popular audience that followed the films of these Egyptian stars. The government of Hosni Mubarak, faced with the grumbling of his national film, feared that it would compete with the national production. The decree n°111 of the year 1987 was then specially promulgated to limit the number of copies of Indian and Pakistani films to five a year and their diffusion time in

---

[5] Interview with Hourriyya ʿAbdin, May 3, 2014 in Cairo.

theaters.[6] This decree reinforces the pre-eminence of Egyptian films in the national territory, since according to the articles of laws 13/1971 and the decree of the Ministry of Culture n°153/1980, theaters must show Egyptian films for at least one week during each season and during the holidays of al-Adha and al-Fitr. Any cinema that shows two or more films simultaneously must show one Egyptian film out of the two shown. In addition, no Egyptian film can be withdrawn from the screens if it brings in at least 50% of the minimum income set by law for each class of theater. Any Arabic-language film that is at least 50% produced with Egyptian capital is considered Egyptian (Ibrachy & Dermarkar 2006, 34).[7] It is important to understand that the 1987 decree came in a context of strong pressure: a very important production of local films (106 in 1985, the year of the release of *Mard*, reaching a peak of 112 films in 1988) after a decade of a low number of feature films and a low number of theaters to accommodate this production. The protection of the Egyptian film with its elective public then almost took the form of a state imperative.

YEAR 2000, STUCK IN SHUBRA, THE IMPOSSIBILITY OF REVITALIZING BOLLYWOOD'S GOLDEN AGE

To get around the 1987 law and to avoid conflicts with the Egyptian film industry, Sobhi found a way around the law: he would screen an Indian film for five weeks, stop for one week, then show an Egyptian film for five weeks, and so on. With a few films under his belt, Sobhi had managed to create a market for Hindi films, and his business was doing well until, in Hourriyya 'Abdin's words "India went crazy" and raised the price of films to $55,000. From that point on, Sobhi feels that the market for Indian film has been in jeopardy. He went to the Indian embassy, as it is the Indian government body that controls the export of films, and told them, "Stop, enough is enough. I made the Indian film. So, you treat me as you treat all the others to whom you sell your films ... It is true that I buy your films, I pay them with the sweat of my brow. I live from that. I

---

[6] This restriction was lifted by the ministerial decree n°388 in 1994.

[7] From Ibrachy & Dermarkar, Report on the Legal and Regulatory Measures Affecting Selected Service Sectors in Egypt, submitted by Nathan Associates Inc. to the United States Agency for International Development (USAID), September 2006. Available online: http://pdf.usaid.gov/pdf_docs/Pnadj736.pdf.

spend a lot of money on advertising."[8] The reaction of the government and/or Indian producers to raise prices in the face of Egyptian success was due to the idea that the profits from their films abroad were escaping them, as local distributors would not transfer the right amount for the films'. Thus, the Indian distributor Gurmuk Singh based in Beirut mentioned a similar controversy at the UNESCO round table in 1965:

> [Gurmuk Singh] then attacks the idea that some people have of the enormous profits made by Indian cinema thanks to these films. He explains that these profits were meager compared to the success obtained. Giving numerous examples, he explains that the largest share of the profits went to local distributors and Arab owners of the cinemas. (Centre interarabe du cinéma et de la télévision 1965)

After this craze, the last film distributed by Sobhi is from 1994, *Dostana* directed by Raj Khosla, with Amitabh Bachchan, and released in India in 1980.[9] It was not uncommon to buy or distribute "old" films since access to films was conditioned by the price of the copies. After this film, Sobhi did not resume Indian films. The embassy tried to renew contact with Sobhi in 2000. He told them, tells us 'Abdin:

> If you want to screen and ensure the return of Indian films to theaters, we need help. We need the help of the cultural attaché here in Egypt. We used to bring back only two prints and for us to do a large-scale publicity campaign, we need at least five prints. We need to have cinemas, like American or Egyptian cinemas, where Indian films would be shown.

The embassy started working on this, and Sobhi went to India, where he bought five recent films. The first film, *Ishq*, was directed by Indra Kumar in 1997, starring Ajay Devgan, Aamir Khan, Juhi Chawla, and Kajol. According to 'Abdin, this film had it all: "It had action, romance, spectacle, and comedy. It was the first time we saw an Indian film with comedy. It was really missing the comedy in Indian films." Before starting public screenings, Sobhi wanted to do a private screening, but from that moment on, the obstacles piled up: no cinema would accept. Even Wassif Fayiz, owner of the Rialto cinema with whom they used to collaborate,

---

[8] Interview with Hourriyya 'Abdin, May 3, 2014, in Cairo.
[9] As in the Greek case described by Eleftheriotis, Indian films arrive in Cairo a-chronologically (Eleftheriotis 2006).

refused, telling them: "You want to organize a private screening? You have to finance it entirely." They used to screen their films at the Shubra Palace cinema in the Shubra district. Yet, in 2000, the cinema did not seem to be up to their standards anymore, as it was located in a working-class neighborhood. At that time, 'Abdin continued, the fashionable cinemas were the ones like Vox, where all the movie-going population went. If someone wanted to see a movie, they went to these cinemas:

> It was impossible for people to set foot in the cinema in Shubra, because the neighborhood was crowded and the cinema was second-rate. So, there was no audience. We wanted to propose to the bigger cinemas to screen in their theaters, with a guaranteed minimum, but we ran into the same problem, they all refused. Why did they refuse? It shows how far the war had come … We didn't lose anything. We had calculated that the weekly goal of the cinema was, for example, 10,000 guineas. We paid these 10,000 guineas. […] Mr. Badi'Sobhi went to see them at the cinema and said: we pay you what you want, you have no right to anticipate how much the film will make, and I take all the losses at my expense. They refused. The film exposed us to the same problems. We renovated our cinema [Shubra Palace], and we did everything we could in the cinema to try to attract customers. The movie didn't work. And the other films, we didn't show them because we couldn't find theaters. The theaters we could show in, it wasn't worth the cost of spending money on advertising […] We wouldn't even pay back the advertising costs of the film. We didn't even earn enough to pay back the price of the film copy. ('Abdīn 2014)

Blocked by the exhibitors, fought by the Egyptian cinema lobby and the political powers, little supported by the Indian embassy in Egypt, endangered by the exorbitant prices charged by Indian productions, Sobhi gave up releasing the four films he had bought. The historical coincidence of Egypt and India's political and social situations that echoed each other in the 1980s, of which Shubra was the epicenter, this favorable conjuncture for the popularity of Hindi films in Egypt faded with the urban mutations and the deployment of multiplexes. With this structural change, the cinema audiences became more middle-class, to whom Indian films were less appealing than Hollywood blockbusters. A snapshot of a pivotal period, *Mard* symbolizes that unique moment when Indian bodies on screen coincide with the bodies of Egyptian audiences.

References

'Abdin, Hourriya. 2014. Interview, Cairo, 3 May 2014.
Aneja, Atul. 2012. India Begins Rebooting Ties with Egypt. *The Hindu*, March 3, 2012, sec. India. https://www.thehindu.com/news/national/india-begins-rebooting-ties-with-egypt/article2957207.ece.
Armbrust, Walter. 2008. The Ubiquitous Nonpresence of India. Peripheral Visions from Egyptian Popular Culture. In *Global Bollywood: Travels of Hindi Song and Dance*, ed. Sangita Gopal and Sujata Moorti, NED-New edition, 200–220. University of Minnesota Press.
Bénard, Marie-Claude. 2016. *La sortie au cinéma: palaces et ciné-jardins d'Égypte (1930–1980)*. 1 vols. Parcours méditerranéens. Marseille: Éditions Parenthèses MMSH.
Bhatia, Shyam. 1977. Indo-Egypt Relations: A Friend in Need. *India Today*, December 31, 1977. https://www.indiatoday.in/magazine/economy/story/19771231-indo-egypt-relations-a-friend-in-need-823976-2014-05-07.
Centre interarabe du cinéma et de la télévision. 1965. *Cinéma et Cultures Arabes. IVème Conférence de La Table Ronde Organisée Avec l'aide Technique de l'UNESCO*. Liban: Beyrouth.
Desai, Manmohan, dir. 1977a. *Dharam Veer*. Action, Fantasy.
———, dir. 1977b. *Amar Akbar Anthony*.
———, dir. 1985. *Mard*.
Desai, Manmohan, and Prayag Raj, dirs. 1983. *Coolie*.
Eleftheriotis, Dimitris. 2006. A Cultural Colony of India. *South Asian Popular Culture* 4 (2): 101–112.
Eleftheriotis, Dimitris, and Dina Iordanova, eds. 2006. *Indian Cinema Abroad: Historiography of Transnational Cinematic Exchanges*. South Asian Popular Culture. Vol. 4.2. Oxford: Routledge.
Ibrachy & Dermarkar. 2006. Report on the Legal and Regulatory Measures Affecting Selected Service Sectors in Egypt. USAID. http://pdf.usaid.gov/pdf_docs/Pnadj736.pdf.
Iordanova, Dina. 2006. Indian Cinema's Global Reach. *South Asian Popular Culture* 4 (2): 113–140.
Kapoor, Raj, dir. 1964. *Sangam*.
Mehra, Prakash, dir. 1984. *Sharaabi*.
Monaco, Eitel. 1966. Exploitation, Distribution, Importation Des Films. In *Les Cinémas Des Pays Arabes*, ed. Georges Sadoul, 164–165. Beyrouth: Centre Interarabe du Cinéma et de la Télévision.
Rao, T. Prakash, dir. 1966. *Suraj*.
UNESCO. 1981. *Importation of Films for Cinema and Television in Egypt: A Study*. Communication and Society 7. Paris: UNESCO.

CHAPTER 11

1985, Amitabh Bachchan's *Mard* in Cairo: Embodying a Transnational Masculinity

Abstract This chapter explores the transnational resonance of Amitabh Bachchan's iconic portrayal in *Mard* within the context of 1980s Cairo, shedding light on the convergence of Indian and Egyptian audiences and the embodiment of transnational masculinity in Bollywood cinema. Despite strict regulations on foreign film exhibition, *Mard* enjoyed a long run in Egypt, attesting to Bachchan's enduring popularity. His embodiment of the "angry young man" archetype resonated deeply with Egyptian audiences, reflecting shared sociopolitical contexts and cultural sensibilities between Bombay and Cairo.

The success of *Mard* can be attributed to a symbiotic relationship between Indian cinema's evolving narratives of rebellion and the shifting demographics of Egyptian audiences, particularly lower-income groups. As Egyptian distributors increasingly catered to these audiences, films like *Mard* captured their imagination, tapping into collective aspirations for empowerment and resistance against oppression.

This chapter delves into the nuanced interplay between cinematic representations of masculinity, societal transformations, and audience reception, highlighting Amitabh Bachchan's role in shaping Bollywood's global appeal and fostering a transnational cinematic dialogue.

Keywords Amitabh Bachchan • *Mard* • Masculinity • Audiences • Angry Young Man • Golden Age

Indian actor Amitabh Bachcan, a global icon, embodies the love affair between Egyptians and Hindi films that began in the 1980s. "*Mard*, I am told ran for 2 years here in Egypt, despite strict rulings on exhibition of foreign films, and because of its cult standing there is a large number that recognizes and adulates Moi," recalls Amitabh Bachchan in a blog post (Bachchan 2015, 2). What brought the Indian actor to the hearts of Egyptian audiences is, I argue, his embodiment of a virility through the figure of the angry young man that shaped Bachchan's stardom. On several levels, the bodily modalities resonated between Egyptian and Hindi cinema, between the bodies of the spectators and the bodies of the actors, and created a popular circuit for Hindi films, hitherto unheard of, to the point of deeply penetrating the imaginary.

Bombay and Cairo, Convergence of Audiences

The success of the film *Mard*, with its political and social tones, can be explained by a convergence of Egyptian and Indian audiences. Set during the British Raj, Mard is the film's eponymous character, a simple *tanga-wallah* (a horse-drawn carriage driver) yet fighting against the British oppressor to defend his people.

In the 1950s, an Indian distributor noted that "The wealthier classes mostly patronize American, English, French and Italian films while the common man goes to see Egyptian films. To the latter, Indian films have the same appeal as Egyptian films" (Birla 1955, 11). From the beginning of the circulation of Indian films in Egypt, it was thought that Indian film attracted a popular audience who were already accustomed to Arab films. This latter idea is based on the notion of a cultural convergence, of shared culture, between these two forms of cinema. This presupposition has an Orientalist bias. Yet, the golden age of Hindi cinema in the late 1980s can still be understood because of this convergence of audiences. In both Egypt and India, the 1980s marked the predominance of popular audiences in movie halls. In both countries, this period saw a significant deterioration in the conditions of cinema-going, causing the middle class to flee.

It was the popular audience that recognized themselves in the vigilante figure of Amitabh Bachchan, a man of the people "angry" against the tyranny of the colonists or the powerful. Around the icon of the "angry young man," the proletarian incarnation of the actor made it possible to identify the bodies of the spectators with the body on the screen. During the 1970s and 1980s in India, the cinema audience became composed more and more of young men from the working classes, while the middle class preferred the domestic comfort of television. While cinema attendance dropped by 50%, the number of television sets increased from 455,000 to 6,750,000 between 1975 and 1985, bringing more viewers to a television soap opera in one evening than to a popular film in a week (Garga 1996, 196). At the same time, the proletarianization of the cinema public in India amplified the phenomenon of desertion of the middle classes and fed their mistrust of cinema. As Aruna Vasudev points out:

> The eighties were the darkest period of the cinema, which, fighting for its survival, resorted to sex and violence to turn viewers away from television and back to theatres. These efforts proved to be counterproductive, as families—the traditional audience of cinema—instead turned away from so much vulgarity and unnecessary violence. (Vasudev 2001, 118)

The same phenomenon occurred in Egypt, where the nationalization policy had a strong impact on the film industry, especially on cinemas and audience attendance. The nationalizations of 1961 reduced private investment and hindered theater renovations. The General Society for the Distribution and Screening of Cinematographic Films, created in 1963, had a project to build 4,000 cinemas—one for each village—in order to "generalize the socialism of entertainment and knowledge" (Mahfouz 1995, 127). But this ambitious goal was never achieved. In fact, the number of cinemas declined steadily. The reduction in the number of cinemas is combined with a phenomenon of desertion of cinemas. After the defeat of 1967, the subsequent banning of most American films, and the retreat to public sector productions that did not always attract the public, the attendance rate collapsed rapidly, from 3.5 film shows attendance on average per person per year in 1960 (i.e., nearly 80 million tickets) to 2.5 in 1966 (65 million tickets) and eventually to one screening every three years, or 19 million tickets (Mahfouz 1995, 126).

It also marks a demographic and audience shift in cinema attendance, as per the words of director Yousri Nasrallah:

> With the great catastrophe of 1967 and the destruction of the cities around Suez, there was an exodus to Cairo, which led to a change in the audience. The great American films had disappeared. In their place, in 1968–1969, we had karate and Indian films. Gradually, cinemas changed their appearance.

As the films were aimed at a much more popular audience, families stopped going, macho language was heard and there were fights. This deterioration affected almost all cinemas: the Rivoli, the Radio and even the Kasr el-Nil, which had switched from United Artists programming to karate films. Only the Metro perhaps ... Cinema in Cairo had become a man's business due to the population explosion and changes in film supply. (Bénard 2016, 190)

In the late 1970s' Egypt, following a similar pattern in India, the deterioration of cinemas further alienated middle-class suburban families from the first- and second-class cinemas in downtown Cairo and Alexandria because of the male and lower-class audience that attended them. This change in audiences reinforced gender segregation in the cinema, as the middle and upper classes, especially women, were prompted to watch films at home, an incentive all the more encouraged by the introduction of the VCR (videocassette recorder).

Egyptian film distributors reportedly paid increasing attention to lower-income audiences since the end of the Second World War, particularly audiences of workers and artisans employed by the British forces who earned enough to make the cinema their primary entertainment. At the same time, directors would have particularly taken these popular audiences into consideration, in their choice of treatment of film scripts, supporting the *happy endings* of their social dramas, as is the case with Kamal Selim's *Les Misérables (al-Bu'asa')* (1943) (Shafik 2007, 302). The height of this demographic change in audienceship peaked in the 1980s. This audience is particularly characterized by its fondness for films starring Farid Shawqi and Rushdi Abaza, stars of the 1950s to 1970s, as the manager of al-Hamra, one of Cairo's oldest and largest video film stores, testified to Viola Shafik in February 2006 (Shafik 2007, 302).

Amitabh Bachchan, the "Angry Young Man" Cult in *Mard*

These structural and sociological changes are reflected in the changing content of Indian cinema. The demand to see masculinity on screen led to the popularity of Amitabh Bachchan. These interconnected developments are key to understanding the success of *Mard* in Egypt. In 1975, *Deewar* (Chopra 1975), consecrated Amitabh Bachchan in the role of the "angry young man." The director, Yash Chopra, usually preferred to tell love stories, distancing himself from the social realism of his brother

B. R. Chopra. However, in the 1970s, anger rumbled and dominated Bombay cinema. In May 1973, *Zanjeer* (Mehra) was released. This film marked the advent of a new type of hero and announced the arrival of the new icon of Bollywood, undisputed to this day (despite a crossing of the desert): Amitabh Bachchan. Impressed by the actor's acting and presence, Yash Chopra wanted to cast him in one of his romantic films, *Kabhi Kabhie*. The financing was already in place, but, excited by a script written by Salim-Javed, the writers of *Zanjeer*, Yash Chopra decided to direct *Deewar*, starring Amitabh Bachchan. The actor owes his character of the "angry young man," or "industrial hero" (Valicha 1988) essentially to the scripts of Salim-Javed. These films, directed by Prakash Mehra (*Zanjeer*, *Muqaddar ka Sikandar*, 1978), G. P. Sippy (*Sholay*, 1975), and Yash Chopra (*Trishul*, 1978) were great successes and remain popular even today.

In Egypt, the film *Mard* condenses around the imagination of a virile people's hero, struggling against political and social oppression. The film is set in the historical moment of early twentieth-century India, under the yoke of the British oppressor. In a mad dash to escape the British, the newborn son of the Hindu king Raja Azad Singh is dropped off by his fleeing parents in front of a temple, where he is taken in by a poor family, unaware of his noble origins. Raju grows up in this home and becomes a fervent defender of the village cause against the British-sympathizing Dr. Harry, who exploits them. Dr. Harry had won a sumptuous house due to his efforts to dethrone Raja Azad Singh.

Eventually, Raju falls in love with Dr. Harry's daughter and finds his father. But King Azad Singh's son is not just any man, he is the very personification of virility, as his name suggests. Mard is the real name of Raju, which his father engraved on the chest of his newborn son with the point of his knife. The child smiled and seemed to feel no pain, while his mother turned her face away from this violent scene. *Mard*, in Hindi, means man, male, even macho. Insensitive to pain, he feels nothing when Ruby, Dr. Harry's daughter, whips him and even rubs salt on his bloody back. He knows how to deal with any problem, and he solves them with his physical and mental strength. When an old woman is dragged to the ground because of a piece of her sari caught in a car wheel, Mard rushes to save her, taking her by the hand. Ruby offers him to become her bodyguard, so that he can have a better social position, but he refuses any submission:

Ruby: No, you misunderstood me. I brought you here for something else.
Mard: If you called me to show me your body, then it's okay, I've seen it *[she receives him in her underwear, lying on a couch, getting a leg massage]*. If there's anything else, it's time to talk business.

- I know your business. You drive your carriage all day. How much do you earn per day?
- No matter how much I earn, it's enough for me. The horse has its feed, I have enough to eat. God does not let me sleep on an empty stomach. We live honorably, without begging anyone for money.
- You sound very arrogant the way you talk.
- Not arrogant, I respect myself. You may be of a higher rank, but we have no less respect for ourselves.
- I like what you say. I want to give you a better status. I want you to be my bodyguard.
- I do not accept your proposal. No matter what his status, a servant must always bow to his master.
- Think about it. I'm not used to being told no.
- If you are not used to being told no, I am not used to saying yes. I may have been born a slave in this country, but my heart has never accepted being a slave, and never will.
- Guards! Stop that man!

Mard's lines, delivered in Amitabh Bachchan's confident and deep voice, are emblematic of the character's manly and moral power. It is through his voice's particular timbre that Bachchan made his mark on cinema. His first role was that of the voice-over in *Bhuvan Shome* (Mrinal Sen 1969). In the skin of the angry young man, he uses his voice to dominate, to show his anger, and mark his intelligence. If the angry young man does not talk about love, he is, on the other hand, eloquent about the exploitation of people by the system. One of Amitabh Bachchan's acknowledged qualities, among other acting talents, is precisely his ability to portray anger. In Javed's words:

People let their guard down in a moment of anger, the true self is revealed. As an actor, Amitabh's anger was never hideous. Other actors mix anger with arrogance. But Amitabh's anger was mixed with hurt and tears. So you accept it, you are fascinated by it, and you find justification for it.

The type of virility proposed by Amitabh Bachchan involves strength of mind and the power of words—served by poetic and intense dialogues of great scriptwriters and dialogue writers. In this cerebral emphasis, it is far from the incarnation of muscular virility of Hollywood actors, based strictly on physical prowess. It is this opposition to American representations of virility that linked Bachchan with the Egyptian actors, if we follow Shafik's analysis. The "machismo of a failed masculinity" (Tasker 1993 quoted by Shafik) as embodied by Sylvester Stallone in *Rambo* (Ted Kotcheff 1983) or Schwarzenegger, where the muscular hyper-virility ends up taking the form of a parody of masculinity, is not found in Egyptian action films. Egyptian bodybuilders with mediocre acting skills, such as Shahhat Mabruk, the hero of many action films in the 1990s, never managed to rise above their status as B-movie actors. On the other hand, Adil Imam, much less muscular and far from a Hollywood-style virility, became the great star of Egyptian cinema in the 1980s. Like Amitabh Bachchan, he became known and popular for his political roles.

While the angry young man of Hindi cinema was born in the context of the state of emergency proclaimed by Indira Gandhi on June 25, 1975, for Shafik the form of masculinity embodied by Adil Imam at the time reflects the political appeasement of the post-Camp David era. It figures, she argues, "the nation's general lack technological advancement [...] not just in a metaphorical sense; for the incapability of producing a perfect 'body machine' runs parallel to the fact that on the structural level the action film posed a profound economic problem for the relatively poor Egyptian film industry" (Shafik 2007, 315). To be precise, "low budgets and lack of know-how in special effects (including make up) kept the Egyptian action film technologically at a quite 'underdeveloped' stage" (Shafik 2007, 315). The Egyptian film scholar reads the figure of Adel Imam as "the parodic insistence on an 'imagined' masculinity; an eloquent inability to successfully acquire technology and physical efficiency" (Shafik 2007, 317). Echoing this, Amitabh Bachchan's physique did not predestine him to become a renowned actor in Hindi cinema: tall, with deep-set eyes, rigid stature, and the somewhat ungainly gait of this slender body, nothing made him the stuff of a hero. Moreover, the combat scenes with his long feet and thin arms detracted from an aura of virile strength. What brought these two heroes, who became rivals on Egyptian screens, to find the hearts of Egyptian spectators might precisely be a common embodiment of masculinity. I argue that the bodily incarnation of a man of the people rebelling against a foreign oppressor gave *Mard* its cult following in Egypt, and embodied Bollywood Golden Age phenomenon.

As the law was restrictive in terms of the number of film copies and consecutive screening weeks in the same cinema hall for Indian films (see Chap. 10), the Bollywood Golden Age phenomenon translated in an exponentially growing VHS (Video Home System) circuit. From the public space of cinema halls, Hindi films entered the intimacy of television homes.

References

Bachchan, Amitabh. 2015. DAY 2541. Tumblr. *Tumblr* (Blog). March 30, 2015. https://srbachchan.tumblr.com/post/115114799301.

Bénard, Marie-Claude. 2016. *La sortie au cinéma: palaces et ciné-jardins d'Égypte (1930–1980)*. 1 vols. Parcours méditerranéens. Marseille: Éditions Parenthèses MMSH.

Birla, M.P. 1955. *Report Indian Goodwill Trade Mission to the Middle East Countries (1954–1955)*. New Delhi: Government of India, Ministry of Commerce and Industry.

Garga, B.D. 1996. *So Many Cinemas: The Motion Picture in India*. Mumbai: Eminence Designs.

Kotcheff, Ted, dir. 1983. *Rambo*.

Mahfouz, Medhat. 1995. Les Salles de Projection Dans l'industrie Cinématographique. In *Égypte, 100 Ans de Cinéma*, ed. Magda Wassef, 124–129. Paris: Éd. Plume: Institut du monde arabe.

Shafik, Viola. 2007. *Popular Egyptian Cinema: Gender, Class, and Nation*. Cairo New York: The American University in Cairo Press.

Tasker, Yvonne. 1993. *Spectacular Bodies: Gender, Genre and the Action Cinema*. Comedia Series. Londres/New York: Routledge.

Valicha, Kishore. 1988. *The Moving Image: A Study of Indian Cinema*. Bombay: Orient Longman.

Vasudev, Aruna. 2001. Le Cinéma Indien. *Revue Des Deux Mondes*, no. 9–10 (October): 116–121.

CHAPTER 12

Shifting Spaces: From Public Cinema Halls to the Privacy of Homes

Abstract This chapter traces the evolution of Bollywood film distribution in the Middle East, exploring the shift from cinema halls to the privacy of homes through VHS circuits and broadcasting channels. Despite political challenges such as Egypt's ban on Indian films and the devastation of the Civil War in Lebanon, Bollywood maintained its presence in the region by adapting to new distribution platforms.

The emergence of dedicated channels like Zee Aflam and MBC Bollywood revolutionized the accessibility of Indian cinema to Arab-speaking audiences, transcending diasporic communities to reach broader viewership. Zee Aflam, launched in 2007, pioneered tailored Bollywood programming for local tastes, while MBC Bollywood, inaugurated in 2013, further expanded the cultural footprint of Indian films in the Arab world. By capitalizing on cable television and digital formats, these channels revitalized the Indian film market in the region, offering a diverse array of cinematic content to audiences amidst the decline of theatrical distribution.

By tracing the trajectory of Bollywood's distribution networks in the Middle East, this chapter offers insights into the evolving landscape of film distribution and consumption, highlighting the resilience and adaptability of Bollywood in the face of changing media landscapes.

© The Author(s), under exclusive license to Springer Nature Switzerland AG 2024
N. Srour, *Bollywood Film Traffic*, Palgrave Studies in Arab Cinema,
https://doi.org/10.1007/978-3-031-64491-7_12

Keywords VHS circuits • Broadcasting channels • Zee Aflam • MBC Bollywood • Bollywood • Middle East

The devastation of the Lebanese Civil War, the consequences of Egypt's nationalization of the cinema industry, and the political ban of Indian film by the Egyptian authorities—all these developments nearly put an end to the circulation of Bollywood films on cinema screens. Yet, Bollywood films had built an audience over the past decades, and people in the Middle East were acquainted with Hindi films. Bollywood films' disappearance from cinema halls did not mean the end of their circulation. It only meant that the film circuits transformed into VHS (Video Home System) circuits and broadcasting channels. As the centrality of the Egyptian and Lebanese market crumbled, Dubai steadily rose to take a central part in the distribution game, changing the whole ecosystem for Hindi film circuits in the Middle East.

BEFORE BROADCASTING, NATIONAL TELEVISION AND THE VHS CIRCUITS

From the Egyptian daily newspaper *Al-Ahram* of May 6, 1985:

> Hindi film in the Egyptian house
> Kamal Al-Shennawi once told me that he was responsible for bringing Hindi film to Egypt. He had bought the film *Sangam* for the sum of 100 guineas to show it in Egypt. But in the meantime the actor Kamal Al-Shennawi was busy with other things, and he forgot about the film. It came back to his mind after a while, and he sold it to a distributor for 60 guineas. He was satisfied with the sale, and especially with getting rid of the film. *Sangam* was shown, and the distributor made exorbitant profits and the public gave it a great reception.
> From that day on, Hindi film has entered the Egyptian market in a big way. I remembered Kamal Al-Shennawi's words about the invasion of Hindi films in the video world lately. Video stores cannot keep up with the popular demand for Hindi films. No Egyptian house is currently short of Hindi films, and the heroes of Hindi films are all known to the Egyptian viewer. Thus, Hindi film has come into competition with Egyptian cinema on the big screen and on video. (Al-Ahram 1985)

In the late 1960s, Egyptian television began to broadcast Indian films on a regular basis (Eleftheriotis and Iordanova 2006; Iordanova 2006).

However, the programming consisted of only a few titles repeated indefinitely, and television was still not widespread among the Egyptian population. "UNESCO estimates put the number of television sets at 57,000 in 1961" (Guaaybess 2013, 120). Films were programmed on the Egyptian national channel, though this was not an official government policy, Viola Shafik points out, since the Egyptian Radio and Television Union did not establish any contracts directly with India. The Indian films shown were negotiated with their Egyptian distributors. According to the recollections of Viola Shafik's informants, the first Indian film shown on television on several occasions was Mehboob Khan's *Mother India* (1957). Under Sadat, Egyptian television continued to show the same Indian films repeatedly until the 1980s. These films were usually broadcasted in the evening, at a time of high audience, or on festivals and holidays. In the 1970s, according to a study on the import of films for cinema and television initiated by UNESCO, Hindi films accounted for a very small segment of foreign films on Egyptian television, around 2% (UNESCO 1981). The arrival of VHS and the golden age of Hindi film, however, marked a turning point. In Egypt in the 1980s, the popular success of Hindi films in cinemas fueled the video market, with the consumption practices of these films being at the interface between the public and private spaces. This was only the beginning of a broader entry of Hindi films into Arab homes.

The Arab space differs from the rest of the world in the early adoption of the domestic practice in film viewing. On the Arabian Peninsula, this provides an adequate solution for women wishing to watch films, since the potential presence of female spectators in cinemas was one of the arguments for banning cinemas in Saudi Arabia.[1] It is not surprising then that the country was among the first in the world to adopt the VCR in the 1970s. By the early 1990s, the Gulf region had the highest rate of VCR ownership, with a higher penetration rate than the United States and Western Europe (Amin 1998, 154 quoted in Mingant 2022, 110). Thus, with television and the VCR, women could access entertainment programs, while remaining within the socially acceptable sphere of private space. The other major argument for the uptake of home viewing was that of security. The Lebanese case is exemplary in this respect, since the Civil

[1] After a long hiatus, the country reopened a cinema in April 2018. Barthe, Benjamin. 'Le cinéma de retour en Arabie Saoudite'. *Le Monde.fr*, April 19, 2018, sec. International. https://www.lemonde.fr/proche-orient/article/2018/04/19/le-cinema-de-retour-en--arabie-saoudite_5287751_3218.html.

War and its bombed cinemas made going to the movies "hazardous if not fatal" (Hollywood Reporter, July 19, 1988, quoted in Mingant 2022, 111). As a result, "most Lebanese opted for the safe environment of their homes to watch videos," especially since the acquisition of VCRs was facilitated by the development of "illegal ports along the Lebanese coast" (Kamalipour and Mowlana 1994, 169 quoted in Mingant 2022, 111). Although exhibitors tried to adapt to the explosive situation in the country, offering film screenings in the morning knowing that the streets of West Beirut were deserted after 5 pm, distributors estimated in the mid-1980s that 50% of the population had lost the habit of going to the cinema (Los Angeles Times, 15 July, 1984 quoted in Mingant 2022, 111). In this context, where domestic practice largely takes precedence over going to the cinema, television offered the possibility for Indian productions not to totally desert the region's screens, while theatrical distribution dwindled in the 1990s in Egypt and Lebanon. This possibility only really took shape in the mid-2000s, with the creation of a 100% Bollywood channel dedicated to the Arab-speaking public, Zee Aflam.

Beyond Diasporic Audiences, Zee Aflam Targets Arab-Speaking Spectators

Zee TV's primary vocation was to reach out to Indian and South Asian diaspora audiences across the world. This objective is consistent with the transnational affiliations that cable channels in general have been able to construct, leading to the emergence of "diasporic communities" and the "restratification of audiences into imagined communities across national boundaries" (Sakr 2001, 7). In this dialectic, the national community—whether inside or outside the nation-state—remains the primary focus. In the case of Zee, targeting the Indian national community required special adjustments. In a country with multiple regional languages, not all inhabitants speak the country's official Indian language, Hindi. The segmentation of channels by region and by regional languages soon became a necessity for the expansion of the Indian media firm. In 1999, Zee launched regional channels, such as Zee Punjabi, Zee Gujrati, Zee Tamil, and so on. The logic of cultural and linguistic adaptation is partly inherent in the logic of the media market in India. These regional channels will then also be offered for the diaspora, which itself is made up of a mosaic of communities. Therefore, when Zee sights were set on the international market, beyond the diaspora audience, it was aware that it had to adapt to the local populations in order to establish a lasting presence there, and thus be able to face formidable competitors seeking to capture the market in the Arab-speaking countries.

> A struggle for influence is underway to capture the Arabic-speaking audience: alongside the Arab channels, a Congressionally funded American Arabic-language channel, Al-Hurra ("The Free") was launched in 2004. France wants to offer an alternative: it plans to launch the French international news channel. (Guaaybess 2013, 13)

To the Arab, American, and French protagonists, we must add India, which already has its eyes riveted on the Middle East region, aware of its economic potential. One of the arguments is the South Asian diaspora established in the Gulf whose banking flows to India are among the largest in the world in terms of volume. However, on the issue of media, studies remain focused on a transnational space within a single region: the Arab world or South Asia. The privileged angle within transnational studies on this topic is, on the one hand, the pan-regional capacity of satellite television channels, pan-Arab or pan-Indian (with an extension to the neighboring countries of India), and on the other hand, their capacity to assert their identity and resist the American media conglomerates. In this case, several works focus on the question of information processing, and in particular on the relationship between the media and democracy.[2] Because of these angles of approach, the Indian cultural presence in the Arab world via a certain number of satellite channels dedicated to Bollywood, although available free of charge via Nilesat and Arabsat, is rendered invisible within the transnational flows.[3]

While Zee does not yet offer a channel specifically dedicated to the Middle East audience, the company physically established itself in the region as of 1998. The Sharjah office, located in the airport's free zone, officially opened on June 1, 1998. Its main activity is the sale of

---

[2] See in particular Gonzalez-Quijano, Yves, and Tourya Guaaybess, eds. *Les Arabes parlent aux Arabes : la révolution de l'information dans le monde arabe.* Arles (France): Sindbad, 2009. Guaaybess, Tourya. *Télévisions arabes sur orbite : Un système médiatique en mutation (1960–2004).* Connaissance du Monde Arabe. Paris: CNRS, 2013.

[3] To be fair, some of these works are based on material that predates the emergence of satellite channels dedicated to Bollywood, even though Zee TV broadcasts to the Middle East as early as the late 1990s and Indian films are part of the program of Arab channels.

advertising space to companies in the Middle East region on Zee TV channels. In the fiscal year 2001–2002, the company moved to another stage, symbolizing the importance of the Sharjah office and the Middle East region to them since 1998. Zee is now broadcasting a dedicated frequency to the Middle East and Pakistan markets in order to increase advertising revenues in the region, allowing companies to directly target the South Asian populations in the Middle East, which was not previously possible (Zee Network 2001, 41). It also increased subscription interest in the channel, which already has a subscriber base of 115,000 as of March 31, 2003, a good start according to the channel's commentators (Zee Network 2002, 34). In the fiscal year 2004–2005, Asia Today Limited invested 100% in Pan Asia Infrastructure Limited (PAIL), whose main activities are broadcasting television channels in the Middle East in South Asian languages and developing Media City in Dubai. As of this year, the office shifted from Sharjah to Dubai (Fig. 12.1).

Fig. 12.1 The office of Zee at the entrance of Media City in Dubai. (Source: Personal archives, photo taken in June 2014 in Dubai)

Fig. 12.2 "We brought Bollywood to Arabia. We are Bollywood." (Source: Personal archives, photo taken in June 2014 in Dubai)

As part of a strategy of global expansion, designed to appeal to local audiences beyond the diaspora, Zee launched Zee Aflam in 2007. By launching Zee Aflam in 2007, Zee was going beyond the diaspora strategy (Fig 12.2). The Arabic name of the channel attests to its targeting of an Arabic-speaking audience, adapting its programs as "a customized beam delivers specifically crafted content catering to the current tastes, likes and needs of the market" of the local population, thanks to a specialized team, while their film and program library is dubbed or subtitled (Zee Network 2008, 22). Zee Aflam is described as follows: "Zee Aflam, Zee Network's Bollywood channel packaged in Arabic for the Arab community," inserted under the umbrella of the Zee MENAP subsidiary for the Middle East region, North Africa, and Pakistan (Zee Network 2009, 7). Its success was not long in coming. In 2009, the channel won an award at the Effies MENA Awards[4] for its marketing in the category "Media/Programs/Internet Service Provider" (Zee Network 2009, 30). The 2010–2011 report mentions that the channel has been number one in the Arab market since October 2008. Among the Asian diaspora, Zee TV remains the number one channel in the UAE, and it was number one during the month of Ramadan in October of the same year (Zee Network 2010, 27 et 29). The success of this channel serves as a benchmark for annual reports and provides assurance that Zee, with the launch of other international channels, is not specifically dedicated to diasporas (Zee Network 2011, 4). In 2013–2014, Zee TV continues to be the number one South Asian channel in the UAE, both in terms of audience and advertising penetration (gross reach point) (Zee Network 2013, 59).

Language is a major issue for a television channel that wants to establish itself in a new market. Zee Aflam has been testing the dubbing of Hindi films into Arabic for several years. While the channel initially began by subtitling the films in literal Arabic, they are gradually being dubbed into Arabic dialects, mainly Syrian. The dubbed films are shown at peak viewing times, in the evening around 9 pm, while the subtitled films are shown in the lower-rated slots. Zee Aflam, as its name suggests, specializes exclusively in films, and is the first cable channel to offer Hindi cinema for Arabic-speaking audiences. As the market grows, Zee decided in 2012–2013 to launch the first general entertainment channel for the Middle East: Zee Alwan (Zee Colors) (Zee Network 2012, 12). Initially specializing in movies, the first point of contact with the Arab population, Zee then diversified into news bulletins and specialized programs by creating the Zee Alwan in 2012. On Zee Aflam, the specialized programs remain related to cinema, with *100% Bollywood* dedicated to cinema news; *Alam Bollywood*, a program dedicated to the cinema industry; or *Look who's talking*, which consists of interviews with Bollywood stars. Zee Alwan presents programs with various themes, including a dance program, *Dance India Dance*; culinary programs such as *Nirmala's Spice World* or *Khonooz Khana*;[5] and Indian *(Okhte Hitler, Nidal Imra'a)* or Turkish

---

[4] Launched in 2004 under the name of GEMAS, the Effie MENA Award aims to recognize the best marketing strategies and practices, across all disciplines and categories, for companies operating in the Middle East.

[5] The above-mentioned programs are part of the Zee's catalogue: produced by the channel in Hindi, they are dubbed or subtitled in Arabic for Zee Alwan.

(The Girl Named Feriha) TV series, dubbed in Syrian dialect. We also find a version dubbed in Syrian Arabic of the *Aladdin*[6] broadcast by Zee Anmol on Zee Alwan, a channel that will be launched later. Zee has also ventured into film production, but this remains a secondary part of its business, which consists mainly of acquiring film content for its multiple branches, with regional language channels in India and around the world. The development of the Zee's chains is, of course, in their economic interest, but the company also develops a cultural argument in its report, an argument that is not found in other regions of the world:

> We are already dubbing our content in various international languages. After successfully offering dubbed content in Indonesia, Russia and UAE, we have launched our second Arabic channel—Zee Alwan. The channel broadcasts some of India's most popular television serials and shows on cookery, travel, health and fitness to the Middle East in Arabic, considering the growing popularity of Bollywood in the Arab world. Our content also strengthens the historic and cultural bond between UAE and India with our offering. (Zee Network 2012, 12)

Zee Alwan is committed to developing a whole series of locally produced programs, in the Emirates and in Arabic, as well as television series that are very successful in the Arab world: Turkish, Syrian, and not only Indian series, while keeping a family content to satisfy its primary audience (Zee Network 2012). The channel is now gradually developing another target audience: expatriates from the United Arab Emirates, with content in English.[7]

With its specific portfolio of three channels aimed at the Arab world, Zee seeks to diversify its audience and reach different segments of the population. While the channel began its presence in the region with a movie channel, the content most familiar to an Arab audience, it later added a general entertainment channel, with shorter programs to attract a new Arab-speaking audience, while an English-language channel now targets a significant portion of the Emirates' population, expatriates, on the

---

[6] It is a television series, broadcast on Zee from November 16, 2007 to March 21, 2009.

[7] A new channel was launched in 2014 in the Arab market—Z Living is dedicated to health and wellness, having first been broadcast in the United States. The channel is available for free, without subscription, from the Egyptian NileSat network.

model of segmentation and niche content. The success of Zee has inspired other channels, whether Indian, such as B4U, or Arab, such as MBC, which compete directly with the pioneering Indian channel in its segment.

MBC BOLLYWOOD, THE ARAB MEDIA MASTODON GOES HINDI

The Saudi media group MBC launched its first Arabic-language satellite channel in 1991, from London, before moving to Dubai in 2002. Indian films were already part of the programming of the group's channels, as MBC used to program one Indian film per week on Tuesday nights on its generalist channel MBC One. On November 27, 2010, the group launched a new channel dedicated entirely to the broadcasting of TV series: Turkish, Egyptian, Syrian, Arab—produced locally in the Gulf countries—but also Indian series.

> This launch is indicative of the niche and audience fragmentation strategy that MBC has been trying to implement for several years now, with the ultimate goal of becoming the leading pan-Arab satellite channel. [...] But more than that, Drama above all marks MBC's desire to confirm the lead it may have in certain sectors in the face of competition that is becoming more diversified and livelier every day, and that is now playing on the same board: the regional, cross-border and free-to-air, and no longer the national state-owned. (Corbucci 2013)

On October 26, 2013, the MBC Group opened a channel exclusively dedicated to Indian film productions, MBC Bollywood. The creation of this channel holds a special place among all the channels of the group. It differs from channels such as MBC Persia (a film channel dubbed in Persian), or MBC Misr, which is specifically aimed at Egyptian viewers, but also from entertainment channels, such as the music channel or the one dedicated to TV series. The specificity of MBC Bollywood lies in the fact that it is a specialized entertainment channel—in cinema—with non-Arabic cultural content—Indian films—but aimed at the Arab-speaking public. The strategy does not involve exploring other markets, but rather building on the local success of a cultural product to offer it to its viewers. Indeed, the presence of Hindi films in Gulf cinemas and the success of Zee Aflam and its large market share must have convinced MBC's management of the great potential of the Arab market for Indian films. The argument, however, is also cultural: "the importance of the family, a patriarchal society and, in short, the same value system" create affinities between the Arab and Indian worlds, as an employee of the channel observed.

The programming strategy is quite different from that of Zee, which began by relying on the South Asian diaspora to grow. For MBC, it is both about convincing a new audience, while trying to "find the audience of over 35 years old who grew up watching Bollywood movies" adds a channel employee. The target audience of the channel is a "young, rather female" audience, considering that Bollywood, as a genre, "offers an idealistic approach to life and the world that corresponds to the vision of the younger generations," the employee notes. This does not deter other segments of the population to try to attract the over-35-years olds by trying to bring them gradually to contemporary Bollywood from the films they have seen in the past or actors they already know. In fact, the channel is in direct competition with Zee Aflam, whose viewers it seeks to attract. In the early days, the press supported the idea that the arrival of MBC Bollywood in the market does not take viewers away from Zee Aflam (Newbould 2014). While the channel started off very slowly at its launch in October with 180,000 viewers, compared to Zee Aflam's 360,000, during the following months the channel scored over 430,000 viewers according to tview[8] figures. In the same month, Zee Aflam had an impressive 700,000 viewers, and the numbers have continued to rise for both channels. Instead of competing, the two channels do not actually cater to the same audience and, in fact, by offering a diversity of content to those interested in Bollywood, they allow more viewers to move from one to the other.

While MBC enjoys a brand image among viewers in the Arab world, with MBC Bollywood it allows this content to be known by the general Arab-speaking public, notably thanks to the announcement of its programs between its different channels, MBC One, MBC Two, or MBC Four. However, the comparison of tview's figures for the years 2013 and 2015 show a different reality in the long run. The arrival of MBC Bollywood on the market seems to be part of a renewed interest in Indian films, as indicated by the arrival of an Emirati audience on the B4U Aflam channel in 2015, where it only reached the South Asian diaspora segment in 2013. Apart from that, it should be noted that MBC Bollywood is

[8] tview is the name of the audience measurement system in the United Arab Emirates.

competing severely with Zee Aflam as the Emirati audience, the audience most interested in the content, is migrating to the Arabic channel at the expense of Zee. The MBC Bollywood channel wins a larger audience share than Zee Aflam, demonstrating both the interest of the Arab audience for Indian programs and Bollywood films, while underlining the flaws of Zee Aflam's marketing strategy, which was a pioneer in the field but probably too much associated with the Indian audience. Through its prestige and legitimacy among the Arab-speaking public, MBC partly gives credibility to the sometimes-disregarded Hindi film.

While the channel is doing well in the Emirates as well as in the Levant countries such as Lebanon, Jordan, and Iraq, the Saudi market presents some difficulties. As a target market for advertisers and publicists due to its high purchasing power, MBC Bollywood is thinking about its content and its program schedule according to the Saudi market. While in the Emirates or Kuwait channel managers easily sign up for the purchase of Indian films, because they are a product the managers are familiar with, to which they have been exposed—either through cinema screenings or VHS—this is less true in Saudi Arabia. Due to the ban on movie theaters, the population has not been made aware of Bollywood before, and the market is in the early stages of product discovery, to quote the firm employee.

The cable channels, with VHS and then DVD, have thus made it possible to continue to make Indian films present at a time when there has been a drying up of theatrical film distribution. Relying initially on a population that is committed to its cultural goods, Zee enters the market through the diaspora, while the multiplicity of channels aimed at Arab audiences today marks the development and growth of the Indian film market in the region. Yet, the proliferation of Bollywood cable and satellite channels makes it all the more complicated for Hindi films to find a way back in Middle East cinema halls outside the UAE.

REFERENCES

Al-Ahram. 1985. *Hindi Film in the Egyptian House*. May 6, 1985, Al-Ahram edition.
Amin, Hussein. 1998. American Programs on Egyptian Television. In *Images of the U.S. Around the World: A Multicultural Perspective*, ed. Yahya R. Kamalipour, 319–334. Albany: State University of New York Press.
Corbucci, Théo. 2013. Drama: MBC officialise le lancement de sa nouvelle chaîne. *InaGlobal*, November 19, 2013. https://www.inaglobal.fr/television/article/drama-mbc-officialise-le-lancement-de-sa-nouvelle-chaine.

Eleftheriotis, Dimitris, and Dina Iordanova, eds. 2006. *Indian Cinema Abroad: Historiography of Transnational Cinematic Exchanges*. South Asian Popular Culture. Vol. 4.2. Oxford: Routledge.
Guaaybess, Tourya. 2013. *Télévisions arabes sur orbite : Un système médiatique en mutation (1960–2004)*. Connaissance du Monde Arabe. Paris: CNRS.
Iordanova, Dina. 2006. Indian Cinema's Global Reach. *South Asian Popular Culture* 4 (2): 113–140.
Kamalipour, Yahya R., and Hamid Mowlana, eds. 1994. *Mass Media in the Middle East: A Comprehensive Handbook*. Westport, CT; London: Greenwood press.
Mingant, Nolwenn. 2022. *Hollywood Films in North Africa and the Middle East: A History of Circulation*. SUNY Series, Horizons of Cinema. Albany: State University of New York Press.
Newbould, Chris. 2014. How the UAE Is Helping Bollywood Boom | The National. *The National*, May 7, 2014. http://www.thenational.ae/arts-culture/film/how-the-uae-is-helping-bollywood-boom.
Sakr, Naomi. 2001. *Satellite Realms: Transnational Television, Globalization & The Middle East*. Londres: I.B. Tauris.
UNESCO. 1981. *Importation of Films for Cinema and Television in Egypt: A Study*. Communication and Society 7. Paris: UNESCO.
Zee Network. 2001. *Zee Annual Report*. 20. Big Ideas in Entertainment. Mumbai: Zee Telefilms Limited.
———. 2002. *Zee Annual Report*. 21. Mumbai: Zee Telefilms Limited.
———. 2008. *Zee Annual Report*. 26. Mumbai: Zee Telefilms Limited.
———. 2009. *Zee Annual Report*. 27. Taking Entertainment Places. Mumbai: Zee Telefilms Limited.
———. 2010. *Zee Annual Report*. 28. Inspired Leadership. Mumbai: Zee Telefilms Limited.
———. 2011. *Zee Annual Report*. 29. 20 Years. Pioneering Vision. Mumbai: Zee Telefilms Limited.
———. 2012. *Zee Annual Report*. 30. Doing More. Mumbai: Zee Telefilms Limited.
———. 2013. *Zee Annual Report*. 31. One World. Mumbai: Zee Telefilms Limited.

CHAPTER 13

Antoine Zeind, Film Distributor in Egypt, "Why Should I Take Risks and [Distribute] a Bollywood Film?"

Abstract "It is not very true that Indian cinema is successful in all Arab countries." This provocative statement by Antoine Zeind, a veteran in the Egyptian film distribution industry, challenges the perception of Hindi films' universal appeal in the Arab world. However, Zeind, with over thirty years of experience in foreign film distribution in Egypt, offers a unique perspective.

As the director of United Motion Pictures, specializing in foreign film distribution, Zeind has played a significant role in Egypt's film industry. His insights into distribution strategies highlight the complexities faced by Hindi films in Egypt's market. Having worked extensively with American film distribution, Zeind offers a comparative perspective on the challenges faced by Indian cinema in Egypt.

Having ventured into Bollywood distribution in the early 2000s, he encountered significant challenges. According to Zeind, Indian producers' reluctance to invest in creating a market for their films in Egypt is evident. Moreover, the rise of cable channels specializing in Bollywood films poses a significant challenge to theatrical releases.

Through Zeind's observations, this interview provides insights into the dynamics of Indian film circulation in Egypt, shedding light on the industry's intricacies and challenges.

Keywords Distribution • Antoine Zeind • Hollywood • Bollywood • Egypt

"It is not very true that Indian cinema is successful in all Arab countries." This sentence, formulated by Antoine Zeind (Cairo, April 2014), sounds like a provocation for those who are aware of immeasurable success of Hindi films in the Arab world. However, the remark comes from a man who has been working in the distribution of foreign films in Egypt for over thirty years. In the early 2000s, he embarked on the Bollywood adventure. He was largely disappointed. Antoine Zeind, today director of United Motion Pictures, a company specialized in the distribution of foreign films, is a historical figure in the film industry in Egypt. As a connoisseur of the market, his description of distribution strategies points out the pitfalls encountered by the distribution of Hindi films in Egypt.

Zeind specialized in the distribution of American films, starting as an employee in the Cairo office of the United Artists Corporation, before later becoming its local director. In 1980, he was appointed as the director of Fox in Egypt. In 1988, he became its agent, and in 1992, Warner's agent for his own firm. His company also distributes from time-to-time foreign films other than American ones. Antoine Zeind knows the different foreign distribution systems in Egypt, Europe, America and, more recently, India. Zeind's plural and comparative vision through his interactions with interlocutors from different countries for the distribution of foreign films in Egypt clearly points out the Indian strategy at the international level. By the admission of this distributor with decades of experience, it is sometimes surprising, if not confusing. The two interviews with distributors Hourriya 'Abdin and Antoine Zeind share the same feeling: it seems to them that Indian producers do not really want to invest in creating a market for their films in Egypt. Not to mention that television, with the rise of cable channels specializing in Bollywood films, is a major competitor in showing the latest films on the small screen. This interview, delivered as a whole, sheds light on all the issues involved in the circulation of Indian films in Egypt, in an organic way.[1]

---

[1] This interview was first published in French under the following reference: Srour, Némésis. '"Pourquoi Devrais-Je Prendre Des Risques et [Distribuer] Un Film Bollywood ?" Entretien de Némésis Srour Avec Antoine Zeind'. In *La Circulation Des Films : Afrique Du Nord et Moyen-Orient*, edited by Patricia Caillé, Nolwenn Mingant, and Abdelfettah Benchenna, 152–59. Africultures. Paris: L'Harmattan, 2016.

Nemesis Srour: You have recently distributed several Indian films in Egypt, although you are primarily specialized in the distribution of American films.

Antoine Zeind I have always liked this kind of films, more as a hobby. During the 1950s and 1960s, they were very successful. If I remember correctly, there was *Mother India* (Mehboob Khan, 1957) and *Sangam* (Raj Kapoor, 1964). A large part of the population even sang *Sangam*'s songs, "*Ich liebe dich, I love you*", this refrain was very famous. Then,[2] there was this Egyptian distributor, Badi'Sobhi, who had two theaters, one in Cairo, the other in Alexandria. He started contacting Indian companies. At that time, Amitabh Bachchan was very well known, and he had come to Cairo once during the film festival.[3] Every week, this distributor showed Bollywood films: one theater in Cairo, one theater in Alexandria, and sometimes two theaters in Cairo in two very popular neighborhoods, in Shubra and in a street called *Šārī'-j-jayš* (the street of the army). In Alexandria, the Odeon Cinema was almost exclusively dedicated to showing Indian films. At the time, Indian films worked mostly with the working class, with students, with a very popular audience, who went to the cinema two or even three times a week. The Indian film had its best period during the 1970s and 1980s. When he died in 2006, his theaters were sold or demolished, and the distribution of Indian film came to a complete halt. There was the occasional Indian film screening once a year, but it was never successful because there was no continuity in the screenings, and there was no cinema that specialized in Indian films.

N.S.: In the 1970s, you didn't think of distributing Indian films yourself?

---

[2] Badi'Sobhi began distributing Hindi films from 1981 (according to an interview with Hourriyya 'Abdin, her director of the distribution office, conducted on May 3, 2014, in Cairo).

[3] For the 15th edition of the festival, in 1991.

A.Z. No, because I am 100% American films. And Indian movies have been a hobby. It's like every now and then you like to buy a whim, drive a convertible sports car, but you never go out and buy it. Yet in Badi'Sobhi's times, during the 1970s and 1980s, Indian film was so successful that a law was passed, or rather a decree was issued: no Indian film could be shown for more than five consecutive weeks. So what was Badi'Sobhi doing? He would screen the film for five weeks, following the decree, and then remove the Indian film. He would show one week of American film, then put the Indian film back on for another five weeks, and so on. To tell you how far the competition with the local film had come. They [the Indian production and distribution companies] didn't take advantage of that. You know, one time when I was appointed director, my boss sent me a note of congratulations, he said, I don't remember verbatim but I remember in general, he said, "Antoine, always remember that the train stops once, if you don't get on you won't get to join it again." So the Indians were very successful during the 1970s and 1980s, they didn't take the opportunity to maintain that success.

N.S.: When did you decide to distribute Indian films?

A. Z. During the film festival,[4] I had the opportunity to meet in Cairo the late Yash Johar,[5] producer of the film *Kabhi Khushi Kabhi Gham*.[6] He invited me to the premiere of the film in London and I happened to have a trip planned for that date. I went there. I attended the private screening of the film, which I liked very much. I felt that the film had an international dimension. It had very big stars. The late Yash Johar was extremely professional with me. He told me, "Antoine, you are known, you have been distributing films for years for Fox, you are an agent for Fox, for Warner. All I want is for the Indian film to be known and propagated in Egypt. I don't want a guaranteed minimum, I don't want to sell the film to you, I don't want anything, all my films are at your disposal for distribution in Egypt." We started with

---

[4] The Cairo International Film Festival (CIFF) in 2001.

[5] Founder of the Indian company Dharma productions, today directed by his son, Karan Johar, director.

[6] Karan Johar, 2001, with Amitabh and Jaya Bachchan, Kajol, Kareena Kapoor, Shah Rukh Khan, Hrithik Roshan.

Kabhi Khushi Kabhi Gham, the success was, I would say, average since we had not distributed Indian films for years. For a long time, I liked these films, I liked the actors, so when I had the opportunity, I went to Mumbai,[7] where I was able to meet directors, distributors, distribution companies. I contacted Eros, Yash Raj, and UTV.[8] Eros was *Krrish 3*,[9] Yash Raj for *Dhoom 3*[10] and UTV for *Chennai Express*.[11] We had these three films, we screened them almost one after the other, but, unfortunately, they were not successful enough.

N. S.: When you say that they were not successful enough, what are your criteria?

A. Z. The number of spectators and the receipts. The Indians think that because their films do well in the Emirates, they will do well in Egypt. But the context is completely different. Oh, and I forgot to tell you that I had the chance, through Fox, to distribute the film *My Name is Khan*,[12] which was a huge success. Seeing this success, almost all the Indian producers contacted me and offered to distribute their films.

N. S.: Do you think that the success of *My Name is Khan*, directed by Karan Johar but financed and distributed by Fox, is linked to the subject of the film or to the fact that it was distributed by the American company?

A. Z. Both, but mostly to the subject. Because in theaters, we saw the reaction when he said, "My name is Khan, I am a Muslim but I am not a terrorist." Everyone was … so word of mouth spread very quickly. The actor is well known, a lot of young people know him, and the fact that it was distributed by Fox, an American company, gave a lot of strength and reasons for the film to succeed.

…But the same question always comes up, and it is asked by exhibitors: why should I take risks and show a European,

[7] August 2013.
[8] Among the most important distribution houses in India.
[9] Rakesh Roshan, 2013 with Priyanka Chopra, Vivek Oberoi, Kangana Ranaut, and Hrithik Roshan.
[10] Vijay Krishna Acharya, 2013 with Abhishek Bachchan, Uday Chopra, Katrina Kaif and Aamir Khan.
[11] Rohit Shetty, 2013, starring Deepika Padukone and Shah Rukh Khan.
[12] Karan Johar, 2010, with Kajol and Shah Rukh Khan.

Bollywood, Pakistani, Japanese film, when I am almost certain that the American film and the local film will bring me x amount of money. Why should I take a risk? And I find that they are perfectly right, because I myself am an operator, I have a cinema in Alexandria, the Amir cinema, built in 1952. It was built in 1952, with a seating capacity of almost 1,500, including the floor and the balcony, and we divided it into 6 rooms. Today, I have 6 films shown in this cinema.

N. S.: How do you explain that Bollywood films are not successful in Egypt today?

A. Z.: What I have noticed is that they [Indian production and distribution companies] don't really want to enter Egypt; or they are interested, yes, but on their terms. You impose your conditions once you are on horseback, but when you are not on horseback, you cannot impose conditions. I told them, in the beginning, you have to make some sacrifices until you reach your goal, then you can impose your conditions. This is what Badi' Sobhi had done at that time, Indian film was playing at percentage, we had a ministerial decree, all films were playing at 50%. Badi' was passing the Indian film at 60, shared between the exhibitor and the distributor. And the cinema was happy. They [the Indian production and distribution companies] did not benefit from this. Yash Johar, rest his soul, wanted to bring in the actors, he wanted to make an exceptional event, and he wanted to invest to do it. Also, in my opinion, in my experience, there is a very big flaw, which maybe Indian companies consider as a quality and I see as a flaw: there are too many satellite channels showing Indian films, and at a very short interval from their theatrical release. While Khan's film *Chennai Express was* being shown, a few weeks later the film was on MBC Bollywood or on Zee Aflam or B4U,[13] I don't remember, but there's not even a six month or a year window. So for the working class, for the students, if I can see the movie at home for free why would I go and pay 50 or 40 pounds?

N. S.: In your opinion, would it be possible to open up the Egyptian market again to theatrical release of Indian films?

---

[13] These cable channels are available free of charge.

A. Z.   All I've learned since I've been in distribution since the 1960s is that there are two ways to work, three to be precise. Either you work on a percentage basis, or you work *flat*: you sell me the film for x amount, I buy it and, profit or loss, it's all for me; or a mixture of both, where you share the revenues above a certain amount. The Indians don't, they want us to pay the cost of the prints, plus the transport, so for a territory that I consider almost virgin for Indian films—distribution almost definitively stopped as I told you at the end of the 1980s—with a gap between 1990 and now, it will be very difficult, for me as for any other distributor, to import Indian films that will work in Egypt. Because you have to pay for the cost of the prints, if you have to put in subtitles as well then you don't have a proper budget to promote the film. When you launch a new film on the market, a French film, a German film, a film of any nationality, first of all you need to have an advertising budget for television, newspapers, magazines; all of this contributes to the success of the film. But if you have a very small budget to make a model or two in the newspapers, in a country of almost 90 million people, not every one of these 90 million reads the newspapers, not everyone lives in Cairo. Moreover, with the law on foreign films, we can only distribute a maximum of 10 copies. And if it's an IMAX film, as *Dhoom 3* is, we are allowed 11 copies. This does not allow you to show the film simultaneously throughout Egypt. So for all films, especially foreign films, American and others, we are focused on Cairo and Alexandria.

N. S.:   What has been your experience in the distribution of Indian films; do you plan to continue your collaboration?

A. Z.:   There was no real understanding between the Indians and us, so as to lead to further distribution of Indian films. We speak a different language. They don't have what Europe has. For example, at the time of Youssef Chahine, the French or the Europeans, not only the French, when they came here during the Cairo Festival Cairo Festival,[14] they wanted the films of Europe to be screened in Egypt. So they supported the films, they participated in the number of prints, they participated in the advertising budget,

---

[14] The French wanted to invest to promote their films in Egypt in 1994.

they even participated in the renting of theaters that screened European and Mediterranean films. In my opinion, this is the way to succeed in penetrating a new territory, at least for the first years. You know there is engagement before marriage, so the engagement has to be successful for there to be marriage, that's what I consider that the Indians have not understood or do not want to understand because they are based on their experience in the Gulf. This is my experience with the distribution of these three films.[15]

REFERENCES

Acharya, Vijay Krishna. 2013. *Dhoom:3*.
Roshan, Rakesh, dir. 2013. *Krrish 3*.
Shetty, Rohit, dir. 2013. *Chennai Express*.

---

[15] Zeind refers to the following films: *Krrish* (Roshan 2013), *Chennai Express* (Shetty 2013), and *Dhoom 3* (Acharya 2013).

PART V

2004–2014. Reconfiguration of Cinema Circuits: Rise and Reborn in Dubai

CHAPTER 14

Ahmad Golchin, The Pioneer: Father of U.A.E Cinema and Indian Film Distributor

Abstract Ahmad Golchin stands as a pioneering figure in the history of the UAE film industry. Founding Phars Film in 1964 in Dubai, amidst a landscape where film activity was nascent in the Gulf, Golchin played a pivotal role in shaping the cinematic landscape of Dubai. Despite initial challenges, including sourcing film prints and garnering interest from producers and distributors, Golchin recognized Dubai's potential.

Golchin's impact extended beyond film distribution; he played a pivotal role in building the exhibition industry in the UAE. From organizing screenings in the desert to spearheading the establishment of cinemas across Al Ain, Ras Al Khaimah, and Ajman, Golchin's efforts culminated in the creation of a robust cinema circuit.

Golchin's legacy extends beyond infrastructure development. He transformed the distribution and exhibition landscape, laying the foundation for a thriving cinema market in the Gulf. His contributions not only fostered the growth of the UAE film industry but also built a real dynamic in the distribution and exploitation of Indian films in the Gulf.

Keywords Ahmed Golchin • Phars Film • Dubai • UAE • Indian Films • Film Industry

"There is one man who can tell you everything about the history of the UAE film industry. He was here when it all began and he's still here carving the way (...) Ahmad Golchin is the man who started things in the UAE. His success and hard work has shaped the industry" (Crane 2011). Golchin founded Phars Film in 1964, in a city where "film activity was still restricted in this sector of the Arab world" (Sadoul 1966, 187). Based in Dubai, a non-place in the geography of cinema, he had to fight for film prints, to interest producers and convince distributors to sell him their films. Yet, he could feel Dubai's potential and people's thirst for entertainment in the UAE (Rai 2021).

Ahmad Golchin is a historic figure of the film industry in the Gulf. The office of his company, Gulf Films, is in the district of Deira, one of the oldest areas of the city where markets and souks of gold, spices, and fabrics are located. Ahmad Golchin arrived in Dubai when he was barely twenty years old. He left his native Tehran in 1963, where he worked in publishing. His business was taking off in Iran, as "the entrepreneur spent a content few years reaping his money through publishing close to 140 books while using the lack of copyright in his favor. However, his luck soon ran out when a few books he published drew the attention of some dangerous people. Fearing for his life, Golchin fled Iran in 1964, using the help of some local pirates to ferry him to the UAE" (Rai 2021).

The port city, still under British rule at the time, was only meant to be a transit city for him and his wife, he tells me. But his papers were stolen, and he was forced to stay there until he could contact the Iranian authorities to renew his passport. The presence of an Iranian on the shores of the Gulf does not seem surprising, given the historical links and exchanges between Iran and the Gulf. Ahmed Golchin is part of the "Iranians [who] built Dubai" (Moghadam 2015, 24) in the mouths of recent Iranian migrants, aware of the anteriority of the Iranian presence. As a result, he obtained Emirati nationality, like many Iranians living in these cities, upon the establishment of the United Arab Emirates in 1971 (Moghadam 2013). However, when he arrived in Dubai, Golchin could not practice his former profession of publishing, since there was no press, or even radio, he says. The only available entertainment was the cinema. As he strolled along the old port one evening, an idea came to him: why not start with films? The books he was publishing were mainstream literature, so there was something in common for him with commercial movies. He bought his first films for 50 dollars, used film prints that he could get very cheaply, mostly Indian, Arab, Persian, and English films.

In the 1970s, he would mainly buy his films from Lebanese distributors:

> Those Middle East film buyers were mainly based in Lebanon, so they were buying movies and distributing it. Maybe more than 80 percent of the buyers were from Lebanon, and 15 percent were from Iran. And the main markets were Beirut and Teheran. They were buying and screening the film in Lebanon, Jordan, Egypt and even Kuwait and Bahrein in standard cinemas. We were buying maybe by kilo because it was used films, they wanted to destroy it so they sold it for very cheap.[1]

One of the successful films, he recalls, was *Hare Rama Hare Krishna* (Dev Anand 1971). This film was shot in two languages, Persian and Hindi. "The Indian version was bad because they tried to dub it and add more sound. The film was a hit in Dubai, and they took it to Kuwait, but the film was censored because of its portrayal of a drug deal" (Golchin 2014). From the copies of Indian films he obtained, he regularly scheduled several screenings per month, once a week. The program sometimes consisted of two films, one American, the other Indian, for example, for the price of a single ticket.

Between 1964 and 1971, he tells me, he used to buy Indian films through the network of gold merchants between India and the Gulf, who brought back with them old films such as *Gunga Jumna* (Bose 1966) or *Mother India* (Khan 1957), and even older black and white films with Raj Kapoor and Nargis. The people of Dubai, Golchin testifies, loved Indian films. One of the big hits of the time was Raj Kapoor's film *Sangam* (1964), which he got within months of its release. During one of his trips to Bombay, he tried to get another landmark film, *Mera Naam Joker* (Kapoor 1970). While he used to buy old and worn-out film prints for 50, 100, 300 or 400 dollars, Raj Kapoor asked for 5,000 for his film. Ahmad Golchin remembers telling him, "There is no real market," and he tried to negotiate, but since it was a big production, Raj Kapoor was not willing to let his film go cheap. Someone pirated it and tried to sell it for $500. Golchin recalls that he told that to Raj Kapoor, who was very angry. "We didn't know there was stealing going on, I mean with the projectionist at the Indian movie nights. When the screening was over, they made copies and sold them in Africa, Bahrain, and Oman."

[1] Interview with Ahmed Golchin, December 14, 2014, in Dubai.

When Ahmad Golchin landed in Dubai in 1964, there was only one cinema, located in Al Nasser Square. "I know that my friend, Ahmad Golchin, would literally carry a reel on his head, take a sheet, set it up in the desert and project his films. That's how he did it," says Avtar Panesar, former Vice President of International Operations at Yash Raj Films (Panesar 2013). It was only the starting point before Ahmad Golchin got involved in building the exhibition industry in the UAE, as "Golchin realized that without cinemas, there would be no one to watch these movies. Which is when he actively also got involved in backing showcasers here, introducing cinemas in Al Ain, Ras Al Khaimah and the Royal Cinema in Ajman. But with the changing landscape and a need for a more sophisticated set-up, Golchin soon became involved in the opening of Deira Cinema, the UAE's first air-conditioned theatre that was inaugurated by Sheikh Rashid himself" (Rai 2021).

Ahmed Golchin's story is in the premises of the film industry in the Gulf countries. With him, the nature of the networks gradually changed. From the circulation of informal film copies and an unheard place in the global landscape of film distribution, he managed to create a real market for cinema. Ahmed Golchin has built a real dynamic in the distribution and exploitation of Indian films in the Gulf.

References

Anand, Dev, dir. 1971. *Haré Raama Haré Krishna*.
Bose, Nitin, dir. 1966. *Gunga Jumna*.
Crane, Kelly. 2011. Father of UAE Cinemas. *GulfNews*, November 30, 2011. https://gulfnews.com/leisure/movies/father-of-uae-cinemas-1.940084.
Golchin, Ahmed. 2014. Interview, December 2014, Dubai.
Kapoor, Raj, dir. 1970. *Mera Naam Joker*.
Khan, Mehboob. 1957. *Mother India*.
Moghadam, Amin. 2013. Un espace social transnational entre les Émirats et le sud de l'Iran : les Khodmouni (Lârestâni) à Dubaï. *EchoGéo*, no. 25 (October). https://doi.org/10.4000/echogeo.13554.
———. 2015. 'Being Persian' au pays des Arabes. *Hommes & Migrations*, no. 1312: 23–30.
Panesar, Avtar. 2013. Interview, Bombay, October, 2013.
Rai, Bindu. 2021. Meet Ahmad Golchin: The Man Who Directed the Birth of UAE Cinemas. *Gulf News*, August 1, 2021. https://gulfnews.com/uae/year-of-the-50th/meet-ahmad-golchin-the-man-who-directed-the-birth-of-uae-cinemas-1.81068530.
Sadoul, Georges, ed. 1966. *Les Cinémas Des Pays Arabes*. Beyrouth: Centre Interarabe du Cinéma et de la Télévision.

CHAPTER 15

Bollywood, the Diaspora and Dubai's Mediatic Boom: The Renewed Conquest of the Middle East

Abstract As Indian cinema sought international markets, Dubai emerged as a pivotal hub due to its media boom, political stability, and South Asian diaspora. Yash Raj Films (YRF), a key Indian player, established a Dubai office in 2004. YRF's strategy focused on direct engagement with local distributors, ensuring optimal screening conditions. This shift mirrors global trends as major firms replace local initiatives, aligning with American majors' models.

YRF's move signifies a broader shift in regional distribution paradigms, aiming to penetrate beyond the Gulf countries. Despite challenges, Dubai's political stability positions it as a launchpad for wider regional expansion. The endeavor faces complexities due to differing market dynamics and a less prominent South Asian diaspora in other Arab countries. Nonetheless, Dubai's strategic location made it a pivotal base for YRF's ambitions to extend beyond the Gulf.

Keywords Bollywood • Dubai • Yash Raj Films • Middle East • Film distribution • Indian diaspora

Indian politics favored a Cairo-centric policy in the 1950s, but as the oil-producing countries grew more powerful, the political and economic focus shifted towards Dubai. The rise of the city of Dubai is part of the broader context of the new importance of the geographical area of which it is the geometric center, "from the Indian subcontinent to Central Asia to the Horn of Africa" (Davis 2007, 62). In the 2000s, the city of Dubai presented solid arguments to make it the ideal anchor for Indian films looking to expand their international market: the media boom in the Emirates, its political stability, and the large South Asian diaspora as Dubai gradually took up the central role for Indian films' distribution in the region, played beforehand by Beirut.

INTERNATIONAL DISTRIBUTION AND THE APPEAL OF THE "DIASPORA MARKET" FOR BOLLYWOOD

The appeal for the "diaspora market" on the part of the Bombay industry occurred in parallel with the Indian government's changing view of its overseas population. This renewed interest is understood primarily around economic and cultural arguments, as the Indian government became aware in the 2000s of the wealth that its diasporas constitutes, an economic but also intellectual and cultural wealth (Bruslé and Varrel 2012, 3). More than twenty million Indians live and produce wealth in over seventy countries. The Bharata Janata Party (BJP) government, which came to power in 1998, therefore sought to attract investment from these expatriates to Indian territory. Aiming to find a solid support base in its diaspora, the BJP government made a decisive change from Nehru's policy of the 1950s–1960s. The country, largely helped by its diaspora to finance its fight for independence, changed its strategy towards its nationals residing in foreign territory in the aftermath of Partition. In the context of post-independence nationalism and the policy of non-alignment, which proposed not to ally itself with either of the two blocs during the Cold War, India developed a Third Worldist claim. Jawaharlal Nehru declared that Indians living abroad were welcome on Indian soil and would be considered citizens of the country if they chose to return. On the other hand, he turned his back on individuals of Indian origin who were citizens of other states. The rise of the Hindu far-right in the 1970s, combined with the crisis in Indian finances that diaspora remittances helped to alleviate, augured a change in the way Indians abroad were viewed. This positive view of the diaspora, through its ability to contribute to the country's growth, was followed by a series of measures, such as the creation of a PIO (Person of Indian Origin) card, which provided customs and legal facilities for people proving their Indian origin. In April 2000, a committee of senior civil servants, academics, and politicians was set up to draw up a report on the Indian diaspora to outline government policy towards them. The creation of the Ministry of Overseas Indian Affairs in 2004 marked the BJP's political will to re-engage with the diaspora, which would be pursued by the Congress government.

For the film industry, producers and film distributors would often rely on Indian settlements abroad to circulate Indian films overseas. In the mid-1960s, a United Nations report noted the difficulties of bringing Indian films to the West, despite the presence of a "facilitating agent" such as the diaspora: "On the other hand, it has not been easy to build up a market in the West. Vested interest has been strong and, by and large, little has been done; the problem of gaining a real foothold remains open" (Toeplitz 1964, 27). However, from the point of view of Indian companies from the late 1990s onwards, a commercial strategy of establishing a foothold in the diasporic markets provides a significant source of revenue, particularly given the purchasing power of these households and the higher price of cinema tickets compared with India, enabling films to become profitable there very quickly. The film industry began to see the full potential of the diaspora market, not only for economic reasons but also because of the prestige associated with these audiences.

Subhash Ghai's film *Taal* marked a turning point on its release in 1998, registering record box-office figures abroad while failing to achieve half its score on the domestic market.[1] Overseas audiences seemed to help Indian cinema by their ability to generate revenue and make a film profitable, unlike the poor and unpredictable mass audience, as per the industry's discourse. From this point on, with some Hindi films achieving greater (economic) success in Britain or the United States, some directors clearly admit to wanting to reach out to the South Asian diaspora audience. In addition to the disproportionate gains from selling tickets in dollars or pounds, gains that are more important at a time when the rupee was constantly being devalued, this audience is perceived as more predictable, according to Ganti's surveys of industry players in Bombay. Often described as a fan of romantic films—with their share of song-and-dance sequences—the overseas territory is sometimes divided into preferences

---

[1] At the same time, *Titanic* (James Cameron, 1998) underscored the importance of the foreign market for Hollywood, leading us to draw a similar mirror image of the Indian and American film industries.

corresponding to regions in India. For example, distributors observed that films that were successful in the cities of Bombay or Delhi also did well in the United Kingdom, the United States, and Canada. Films that are successful in Punjab do well in the Gulf (Ganti 2012, 291). With one difference, only blockbusters with star actors in the cast penetrate the overseas market.

When it comes to international distribution strategy and the Arab market in particular, Yash Raj Films (YRF) is a pioneer and presents a unique vision. In the Indian cinematographic landscape dominated by Bombay cinema, YRF is a reference company, as it has brought to the screen some of the greatest commercial and popular successes of the last forty years. Closely associated with the trajectory of the man who founded it, director Yash Chopra, Yash Raj Films infuses Hindi cinema with a romanticism and pure sensuality that lend this commercial cinema its distinctive appeal and credentials. Yash Raj Films was founded on September 27, 1971, the date of Yash Chopra's 39th birthday, "in his office in Shantaram's studio, Raj Kamal in Parel (where he stayed until opening his own office around the time of *Silsila*, 1981), and the release of its first film on 27 April 1973," writes Rachel Dwyer (2002, 55). The director forged his style from his first film, *Daag* (1973), a commercial and critical success. The film made a lasting mark on the landscape of Hindi cinema by offering central roles to one of the greatest stars of Indian cinema, Amitabh Bachchan. He directed two of the films that marked the actor's career: *Deewar* (1975) and *Trishul* (1978). The meteoric rise of the character of the "angry young man" marked the 1970s and 1980s and was followed in the 1990s by the return of romantic comedies. Yash Chopra and his son Aditya Chopra directed some of the most iconic films of this decade, featuring the inescapable duo of actors: Shah Rukh Khan and Kajol. At the turn of the 2000s, the company tried a new genre and produced the *Dhoom* series, action films and crime thrillers, emblematic of the young and urban middle-class culture of the big cities.

In 1995, Yash Raj Films produced *the* film that marked a breakthrough in the economic and aesthetic history of Hindi cinema, *Dilwale Dulhania Le Jayenge* with Aditya Chopra making his directorial debut. For the first time, the character of the Non-Resident Indian (NRI) makes its appearance on screens. The film poses the inescapable antagonism between tradition and modernity, through the forbidden love story between Raj and Simran, while she is promised to another man, in India. The film shattered all records at the Indian box office, and the film remained in theaters in Bombay for more than 20 years at the Maratha Mandir cinema. When the company decided in 2015 to stop showing the film, fans opposed it, organized a protest, and obtained that the film remain scheduled, till today (Bhatti 2015). Beyond this undeniable record, the film marks a turning point in foreign markets with its impromptu success and the largest box-office receipts to date in foreign territories. The film opened eyes to the economic power of the diaspora and from then on, the company had its eyes set on the international market. To this end, Yash Raj set up a distribution branch to control the distribution of his films and launched a merciless battle against pirates. Only two years after *Dilwale*, the company opened its first branch in London in 1997, then expanded to New York in 1998, in search of the famous "diaspora dollar" (FICCI-KPMG 2014). A series of films produced by the company were able to achieve considerable success in these markets, to the point that Yash Chopra claimed in 2006 that Britain was their number one market (Athique 2008, 708). As a result, because of the importance of foreign markets, the company has become more sensitive and uncompromising about pirate copies of its films:

> Yash Raj Films has instigated increasingly frequent raids and legal proceedings against the pirate trade, and publicizes these activities on their website, following a policy of 'naming and shaming' outlets that they have prosecuted for stocking counterfeit Yash Raj titles. This serves 'as a warning that the Indian film and music industry intends to aggressively prosecute companies and individuals that engage in piracy. In recent years Yash Raj has been involved in raids in the US, the UK, the Netherlands and Australia, seizing hundreds of thousands of illegal DVDs. The reasons for this international effort are clear, since Yash Raj Films estimates that it loses $5 to pirate sales for every $1 of legitimate sales'. (Athique 2008, 708)

Obviously, the high profits of films in these markets, relative to the exchange rate and retail price, make producers even more intransigent on the pirate issue. In addition, the copyright laws of these Western countries allow for the effective prosecution and conviction of pirates, whereas this is comparatively more difficult in some African and Asian countries where the smuggling of Indian films is rampant (Athique 2008, 708).

In a few years, the development of the company's distribution arm has placed it among the largest international companies. According to a survey conducted by the American magazine *Hollywood Reporter* on the largest film distribution companies in 2004, Yash Raj Films Studios was ranked twenty-seventh in the world, the largest distribution company in India. The company meets other major players in the international market, such as Eros International, founded in 1977 by Arjan Lulla, and UTV Motion Pictures, established in the 1990s by Ronnie Screwvala and which became a subsidiary of Disney in 2010. The Eros company, of which Arjan Lulla is today the honorary president, began operating informally, obtaining pirate copies at first, until the legal acquisition of exploitation rights for films from one of the largest catalogs on the market (about 3,000 films of all types of exploitation rights). Ronnie Screwvala is one of the most influential figures in the Indian media industry. He has participated in the installation of cable channels in the country, in the development of the global Indian film market by drawing inspiration from American financing models, while being a producer on numerous films, both in the Bollywood industry (such as the film *Chennai Express* with Shah Rukh Khan released in 2013), and "auteur" films, such as *Fashion* by director Madhur Bhandarkar released in 2008. These two companies are also investing in Gulf cinemas by distributing their films there, yet without setting up a decision-making branch. They operate from their headquarters in Bombay, relying on local agents in Dubai, such as Gulf Films and Al Mansoor. In fact, Yash Raj Films is the only Indian company to operate directly from the UAE territory.

Yash Raj Films, a Unique Vision in International Distribution

Placing itself in a hegemonic position on the Indian territory, controlling the production and distribution of its films, Yash Raj has followed the model of vertical concentration. The interest of this concentration allows for an increase in profits and to gain greater control over the circulation of films. From this perspective, the Dubai and Gulf market is at the crossroads of a double challenge: to establish a legitimate circulation of films in a space where the informal economy of Hindi films was dominant, and to regain control of a circuit at a time when the media industry in the Emirates was in full effervescence. In 2004, Yash Raj Films opened a branch office in Dubai, following its dynamic of setting up and increasing its presence in the foreign market. The arrival of Yash Raj Films may seem late in comparison to the Lebanese firm Empire, which set up shop in 1998, but the latter is largely a pioneer in the Bombay industry. YRF is the only firm to have opened an office in the Emirates, and has already been established for 10 years, while reports to the Indian film industry are still encouraging the exploration of the Middle Eastern market as if it were a discovery in 2014:

> It is time for Indian companies in the M&E sector to begin looking at opportunities outside India. While several companies have gone overseas in search of the diaspora dollar, there are opportunities that Indian companies could begin to explore in mainstream markets overseas. For example, Africa and the Middle East are some of the fastest growing M&E markets. As companies in other sectors have shown, the experience of working in India is an asset when entering these markets—Indian M&E companies could do well to explore the MEA region. (FICCI-KPMG 2014 Foreword)

The meeting between Dubai and Bombay was made possible by economic policies that, on both sides, allow the expansion of the film market: the 1991 reform in India and the will to prepare the post-oil era in the Emirates translates into a massive investment movement in the media industries for Dubai. For Yash Raj Films, the confluence of cutting-edge cinematographic structures and a large South Asian diaspora in the Gulf countries made it an ideal market, particularly sensitive to the distribution of Indian films. The Indian company adopted an expansion strategy based on a world map that essentially distinguishes two types of markets, defined as follows by Avtar Panesar, former vice president of international operations:

> The traditional markets concern the regions of the world where Indians live. Indians, Pakistanis, Bangladeshis. Anyone who watches Indian films, understands the language, the diaspora market so those are the traditional markets. Or at least we consider them a traditional market. What is not traditional for us is where they don't speak the same language but are willing to watch these films, like Germany, or even France, Korea, Peru or Japan. Those are not traditional markets for us. And those are the ones we are trying to develop. (Panesar 2013)

In the distribution of Indian films in the region, the countries that make up the Gulf Cooperation Council, with the exception of Saudi Arabia, are considered the primary markets. Countries such as Egypt, Lebanon, Jordan, Iraq, and Syria are peripheral, and considered "non-traditional markets" because it is not possible to show every Bollywood film there, only the ones starring a Khan in it, a Shah Rukh Khan or an Aamir Khan.[2] The mental map of worlds where Arabic languages are in the majority unfolds in concentric circles in the vision of international distribution for YRF. The Gulf countries, in the first place, because of the strong presence of the diaspora; the Middle East, a territory to be conquered but difficult at that point in time because of the war in Syria; North Africa, and Morocco in particular, where they are also trying to expand but which requires a mastery of the French language; Pakistan, which is also under the responsibility of the office set up in Dubai, and which appears to be an important market for their films. Films broadcasted in the Gulf are subtitled in English and Arabic, and it is the Arabic subtitles that will be used in the rest of the region.

YRF's Strategy, Establishing a Strong Foothold in Dubai

However, the establishment of a local presence was a major challenge for Yash Raj Films given the anteriority and hegemony of Phars films on the Bollywood film market in the region. The strategy adopted by Yash Raj in the field consists in regaining control over the circuits and modalities of theatrical distribution of their films. Until now, the intermediary and local agent for the distribution of the company's films in cinemas was the Grand Cinemas chain, owned by the distribution company Gulf Films. Ahmed Golchin, a partner of Gulf Films, was also the first contact person for Yash Raj Films in the UAE. In view of the market potential, Yash Raj Films was willing to create the best conditions for its movies. Grand Cinemas would not screen several Indian films simultaneously in the same cinema, which meant that the films had to be shown one after the other, for one or two weeks each, preventing the films from getting their maximum return at the box-office.

---

[2] The three best-known Khans, who are not related despite the common surname, are actors Salman Khan, and his role as a policeman in *Dabangg* (Abhinav Kashyap, 2010); Shah Rukh Khan has acted in films that have marked the history of Indian cinema, such as *Dilwale Dulhania Le Jayenge* (Aditya Chopra, 1995), *Kabhi Khushi Kabhi Gham* (Karan Johar, 2001), and *My Name is Khan* (Karan Johar, 2010). The third, Aamir Khan, is known for acting in "serious" films, such as *Lagaan* (Ashutosh Gowariker, 2001) and *Taare Zamin Par* (Aamir Khan, 2007).

I went out on a limb really in 2004 when I went there and basically went to war with them and said, 'I'm not going to give you my biggest movie of the year unless you do it my way'. Obviously, they weren't happy about it. I had to release the film, in one cinema in Dubai. Six months later, everyone understood what I was getting at, and we became friends again. (Panesar 2013)

The establishment of an office in Dubai allowed Yash Raj Films to be in direct contact with the local distributors and exhibitors and to discuss directly the rules for the distribution of its productions: multiple and regular screenings, a maximum number of screens in several multiplexes, and the guarantee to leave the film on the screen until the tickets run out. The objective was both to consolidate the presence of YRF films in the Gulf countries, to become the privileged interlocutor for Indian companies who wanted to distribute their films in the region, and to expand its distribution. This strategy confirms the paradigm shift in film distribution in the region: the increasing integration by large firms, on the model of the American majors, is replacing local and discontinuous initiatives (Mellor et al. 2013, 188).

While there is a potential market, particularly because of the large South Asian diaspora, but also among local populations, the challenge at the heart of this establishment was a marketing strategy that could compete with the huge sums of money that American firms were able to release to visually flood the urban space. In Hollywood, economic strategies are accompanied by cultural strategies. To take up Nolwenn Mingant's analysis, thinkers of American imperialism evaluate the Hollywood film as an enterprise of expansion of American values, in particular of the consumer society. For many researchers, the dominance of Hollywood firms is explained by their universalism, while for Scott R. Olson, it is thanks to their "narrative transparency" that American films find an echo in every culture. Another angle of analysis is a seduction operating for commercial rather than political purposes: "the central question that the majors ask themselves is the following: how to make spectators from all over the world want to see Hollywood productions? The creation of the desire to see is thus the central mechanism by which the cultural strategies of the majors are defined here" (Mingant 2010, 75–76). Marketing, which is concerned with how to seduce the public, considering the recipients of its message, is difficult to establish at the international level, and requires a locally adapted strategy. Thus, in the case of cinema, Hélène Laurichesse

Fig. 15.1 Godzilla poster along Sheikh Zayed Road

speaks of "cultural marketing" (Laurichesse 2006). Faced with the gargantuan positioning of Hollywood firms, the marketing strategy of Indian companies is completely invisible. We find this first of all, in the urban space, if only in Dubai, where the majors are able to display posters several meters long for the advertising of their film. When I was there in 2014, the poster for the film *Godzilla* was spread out in a grandiose fashion along the central artery, Sheikh Zayed Road (Fig. 15.1). To suspect the presence of an Indian film, you had to get to the theater itself: there, films from India appeared in the lobby with the screening times (Fig. 15.2). Only, no poster of a Bollywood or Kollywood film is present next to those of American films which are spread out in all the spaces of the cinema (Fig. 15.3). The Indian film poster is only displayed at the entrance of the room where the film is shown, making a poor showing compared to the visual overabundance of Hollywood films (Fig. 15.4).

While Indian films seem far from being able to compete with Hollywood, the company, Yash Raj Films, is looking to expand the market in the region, beyond the Gulf countries where they are well established. The United Arab Emirates has the advantage of political stability, which makes it possible to coordinate the distribution of films to the rest of the region. Dubai then serves as a base to extend the distribution of films to the rest of the region, which presents the double challenge of not being as

Fig. 15.2 Display of movies screening times inside the cinema

Fig. 15.3 Hollywood blockbuster posters in a Dubai mall

Fig. 15.4 Hindi film poster inside a cinema in Dubai. (Source: Personal archives, photos taken in May 2014 in Dubai)

politically and economically stable, and of forming a "non-traditional market" since the presence of the South Asian diaspora is not as influential as in the Gulf countries, to use the analytical categories of the Indian studio. Reconnecting with a golden age of Hindi cinema, recreating the enthusiasm of Middle Eastern populations for these films, however, appears to be an arduous task in the 2010s, as is demonstrated by the *Dhoom 3* attempt of 2013.

REFERENCES

Athique, Adrian. 2008. The Global Dynamics of Indian Media Piracy: Export Markets, Playback Media and the Informal Economy. *Media, Culture & Society* 30 (5): 699–717.

Bhatti, Sharin. 2015. 1 009-Week Run Proves Too Short for Fans of DDLJ Bollywood Classic. *The Guardian*, February 27, 2015, sec. Film. http://www.theguardian.com/world/2015/feb/27/protests-prompt-return-to-indian-cinema-of-film-that-ended-run-after-1009-weeks.

Bruslé, Tristan, and Aurélie Varrel. 2012. Introduction. Places on the Move: South Asian Migrations through a Spatial Lens. Edited by Tristan Bruslé and Aurélie Varrel. *South Asia Multidisciplinary Academic Journal*, no. 6 (December). http://samaj.revues.org/3439.

Davis, Mike. 2007. *Le stade Dubaï du capitalisme*. Penser, croiser. Paris: les Prairies ordinaires.

Dwyer, Rachel. 2002. *Yash Chopra*. World Directors Series. Londres: British Film Institute.

FICCI-KPMG. 2014. The Stage Is Set. [online https://www.kpmg.com/IN/en/IssuesAndInsights/ArticlesPublications/Documents/FICCI-KPMG_2015.pdf]: Indian Media and Entertainment Industry Report. https://www.kpmg.com/IN/en/IssuesAndInsights/ArticlesPublications/Documents/FICCI-KPMG_2015.pdf.

Ganti, Tejaswini. 2012. *Producing Bollywood: inside the contemporary Hindi film industry*. Durham: Duke University Press.

Laurichesse, Hélène. 2006. *Quel marketing pour le cinéma ? Cinéma & audiovisuel*. Paris: CNRS éd.

Mellor, Noha, Khalil Rinnawi, Nabil Dajani, and Muhammad I. Ayish. 2013. *Arab Media: Globalization and Emerging Media Industries*. John Wiley & Sons.

Mingant, Nolwenn. 2010. *Hollywood à la conquête du monde: marchés, stratégies, influences*. In *Cinéma et audiovisuel*, vol. 1 vols. Paris: CNRS.

Panesar, Avtar. 2013. Interview, Bombay, October, 2013.

Toeplitz, Jerzy. 1964. Indian Films and Western Audiences. WS/0764.102-CUA. Paris: United Nations Educational, Scientific and Cultural Organization. UNESCO.

CHAPTER 16

2013, Distribution Beyond the Gulf: The *Dhoom 3* Attempt

Abstract Against the backdrop of declining theatrical distribution for Hindi films in Egypt and Lebanon during the 1990s, this chapter delves into Bollywood's endeavor to attract audiences to theaters and compete with Hollywood productions. Focusing on Yash Raj Films' strategy in 2013, it explores their efforts to penetrate markets beyond the Gulf region. Despite relying on the South Asian diaspora in the Gulf as the primary audience, the Middle East film market posed a unique challenge due to its limited Indian community. However, leveraging its Dubai-based presence since 2004, Yash Raj Films established a distribution strategy in the region.

The international release of *Dhoom 3* in December 2013 marked Yash Raj Films' foray into new Middle East and North Africa territories, beyond its traditional Gulf stronghold. However, venturing into the Middle East presented its own set of challenges, where competition from Hollywood, Arab cinema, and television was fierce. Yash Raj Films' initiative aimed to tap into untapped markets outside the Gulf's saturated arena.

Keywords Yash Raj Films • Middle East • *Dhoom 3* • Film distribution • Bollywood • Gulf

© The Author(s), under exclusive license to Springer Nature Switzerland AG 2024
N. Srour, *Bollywood Film Traffic*, Palgrave Studies in Arab Cinema, https://doi.org/10.1007/978-3-031-64491-7_16

After the decline in theatrical distribution for Hindi films in Egypt and Lebanon during the 1990s, Bollywood distributors faced the challenge of attracting audiences to the theaters and competing with Hollywood productions. The Indian company Yash Raj Films (YRF) set up to tackle this challenge in 2013. While it relied on the South Asian diaspora as the primary audience for its films in the Gulf, this strategy was not viable for the Middle East, which has a very small Indian and South Asian community (around 500 Indian families in Egypt and 8,000 Indians in Lebanon). Yet, with a Dubai-based office since 2004, YRF has built up enough network links in the region to establish a distribution strategy beyond the Gulf countries.

Dhoom 3, The Chosen One to Rekindle the Flame

Dhoom 3 (Vijay Krishna Acharya, 2013), the latest installment in the *Dhoom* series (which began in 2004), stars actor Aamir Khan, who inherited the lead part, after John Abraham and Hrithik Roshan in *Dhoom* (Gadhvi, 2004) and *Dhoom 2* (Gadhvi, 2006), respectively. This action film, combining police investigations and large-scale musical sequences in an urban setting, is part of a stylistic movement that follows the socio-economic mutations of a post-liberalization India. It is a film aimed at the urban middle-class youth who consume cinema in the multiplexes proliferating across India. It is a kind of film that aims to compete with Hollywood through the technical means it employs, while retaining its "difference." According to Yash Raj Studios, this is the kind of added value to be defended on the film industry market.

For the company, the release of this film was a technological event—the press promotion of the film emphasized the use of Dolby Atmos sound technology, used for the first time by the studio, which was modernized for the occasion—as well as a political and economic one. The film was released only in digital form on screens in order to control pirate copies and avoid the losses associated with this informal market. This choice directly endangered the Indian operators of single-screen cinemas, equipped only with 35 mm projectors, whose viability depends on commercial films like Yash Raj's, their success in theaters being virtually guaranteed. It was also a strategic event on an international scale since the aim was to achieve simultaneous distribution in as many countries as possible. By way of comparison, it was in the early 1990s that the notion of day-and-date release was imposed on the Hollywood majors, in order to transform the release of big-budget films into a global phenomenon through a "global communication" operation (Mingant 2010, 226). In India, "the fight against pirates, who can intervene at various points in the exhibition process (between editing and the delivery of the film to the cinema), obliged distributors in the 1990s to organize the release of the film at the same time in all cinemas in the country (All India Release)" (Grimaud 2003, 435). The international release of *Dhoom 3* took place simultaneously on December 20, 2013, in England, Australia, France, India, and New Zealand. In the Middle East region, where the film was released with a slight delay, it marked the company's first release outside the perimeter of its primary and traditional markets.

Similarly, Karan Johar's 2010 film *My Name Is Khan* was distributed in the region to phenomenal success. Produced by the Dharma Productions studio owned by the director himself, the film's Egyptian release was facilitated by the Lebanese Empire network circuit and by Antoine Zeind's company, United Motion Pictures (UMP). Ninety percent of the film's profits were made on the foreign market, and it earned over $500,000 in Egypt, over $60,000 in Lebanon, and over $2 million in the United Arab Emirates. However, the film was co-produced by 20th Century Fox, in charge of international distribution in partnership with the private Indian channel Star. Fox Star Studios, in charge of distribution in India, is a joint venture between 20th Century Fox and Star, an Indian company that has become a Fox subsidiary. The American company's links with the Lebanese network explains the showing of this Indian film in Beirut.

Empire is one of the historic players in the Lebanese film industry, on an international level. Historically, Empire cinemas managed international releases from early on. In 1954, the chain was able to manage simultaneous film releases with London, Paris, and New York. Gradually, Empire established itself as the main and exclusive distributor for a number of Hollywood majors. In 1958, the company won exclusive distribution rights for United Artists films in Lebanon and Kuwait. In 1964, when Columbia Pictures closed its offices in Beirut, it appointed Empire as exclusive distributor for the Middle East. In 1988, Empire became 20th Century Fox's exclusive distributor in Lebanon and the Gulf.

The American production of the Indian film *My Name Is Khan* makes it a singular object in the context of Indian film distribution in the region, as the film's release benefited from powerful patronage and the network of one of Lebanon's oldest exhibition and distribution companies. Empire boasts about it on its website:

2010—Unprecedented records
Empire International distributed three films that broke ALL box-office records throughout the Middle East. *My Name is Khan*, an Indian Fox Star production; 2012, Roland Emerich's cataclysmic apocalypse produced by Columbia; and, last but not least, *Avatar*, the unrivalled performance release that set the bar for years to come. Together, these three films brought in almost two million spectators in the Middle East.[1]

Similarly in Egypt, Antoine Zeind's United Motion Pictures (UMP) was the American company's local agent. Prior to *Dhoom 3*, the film *Chennai Express* (Rohit Shetty, 2013) distributed by UTV Motion Pictures, had been released locally in Egypt by Antoine Zeind, head of United Motion Pictures, who planned to release a trilogy of Indian films in succession.

The establishment of other local players presents major obstacles to the return of Indian films to screens in the Levant. Between Hollywood, Arab cinema, and cable channels specializing in Indian cinema, such as B4U, MBC Bollywood, and Zee Aflam, competition took different forms. Competition from television plays an essential role in Egypt, according to distributor Antoine Zeind, since it diverts a low-income audience—the preferred audience for Indian films during their golden age—away from cinemas. As for multiplex audiences in both Egypt and Lebanon, they prefer American and Arab films to other production. On the contrary, former vice president of international operations at YRF, Avtar Panesar, sees television as a means of getting viewers used to Indian films in the same way that pirate networks have enabled markets to develop, as Adrian Athique demonstrates (Athique 2008). However, even the sale of pirate DVDs of Indian films has largely dried up in Lebanon, testifying to a decline in interest and demand for this cinema. This trend has made Yash Raj Films' strategy an attempt to open up a kind of "new" territory for Bollywood movies.

Opening "New" Territories Outside the "Saturated Market" of the Gulf

While *Dhoom 3* was released in a region familiar with Hindi films, its release on December 26, 2013, marked the start of a strategy of conquering "new" territories for the Indian studio, which until then had not ventured beyond the conquered terrain of the Gulf.

---

[1] Empire Theatres—History, www.empire.com.lb/AboutUs/History, accessed December 9, 2015.

While Hindi cinema easily dominates screens in Northern India and has an important presence in South Asian countries as well, in the Gulf, it faces competition from Tamil or Malayalam films, where the migrant population is predominantly from Kerala, a Malayalam-speaking state in South India. The United Arab Emirates appears to be a saturated market, where Yash Raj Films faces competition not only from Hollywood but also from regional Indian film productions, other than Bollywood. It becomes all the more important to establish a presence elsewhere in the Middle East and North Africa (MENA) zone, a logic already initiated by the Empire network of cinemas. Gino Haddad, the company's CFO, says: "We're looking for opportunities throughout the region, with the exception of Dubai, where the market is saturated." According to Haddad, Erbil, the capital of the Kurdistan region in northern Iraq, offers a number of advantages: "it's a completely virgin market, in terms of cinema, but also entertainment in general, as well as being very stable," an advantage that seems to be undermined by the recent presence of the Islamic State in the region. The group was even considering two other projects in Kurdistan, in Suleimania and Dohuk.

Dhoom 3 was released simultaneously in a network of cities in the region, with Yash Raj Films' aim of opening up a new market from the Middle East to North Africa. Due to the war in Syria, the film could not be shown there, but it was on screens on December 26, 2013, in Beirut and Amman, on January 1, 2014, in Cairo, and the following day in Erbil. Yet, the Indian company's regional expansion faces structural obstacles: the lack of screens and cinemas throughout the MENA zone. Outside the Emirates, the two most important markets remain Egypt and Lebanon. The UAE, Egypt, and Lebanon have the largest number of screens in the region; together, they account for more than half the total number of screens in the MENA region. Egypt, on the other hand, has one of the lowest ratios of screens per inhabitant, with cinemas concentrated mainly in two cities and a large population scattered throughout the country. Lebanon has the highest ratio, partly explained by its dense population and the purchasing power of its inhabitants. Apart from these three countries, and with the exception of Qatar, the number of screens and cinemas is very low in the other countries in the region, presenting little market potential. Figures clearly explain the decision, from an economic point of view, to focus primarily on Egypt and Lebanon, even if Yash Raj Films is keeping in mind other countries in the Arab region, and Morocco in particular, because of its affinities with Bollywood content. In addition to the economic and structural aspects, and the considerable geopolitical instabilities in the region, with the war fronts in Syria and the Islamic State, the Bombay industry also has to adapt to local audiences with cultural marketing strategies.

In order to appeal to Arabic-speaking audiences, the film's title song was recorded by Lebanese singer Naya. Naya released her first single in 2009, and when Yash Raj Films contacted her, she had just released her first album, *Mandam*. She was considered a rising star in the Arab-speaking world who could attract a young audience. What is more, Indian producers were advised to choose a Lebanese singer, with lyrics in Lebanese dialects, because of the country's dynamic music industry that appealed widely to Arab-speaking audiences, beyond Lebanon. While Antoine Zeind handled distribution in Egypt and struggled to find multiplexes willing to show the film, it was the Empire network that coordinated with Yash Raj's office for the release throughout Lebanon, and in its new complex in Erbil. By setting up in Dubai, the company was seeking to diversify its local agents. The cooperation with the Empire network enabled the company to team up with an experienced local firm, while exploring other distribution networks. While the film topped the box-office charts on release and remained in theaters for over eleven weeks in India, it was only released for one week in Lebanon, where it ranked twelfth in a box-office dominated by Hollywood productions but remained in theaters for three weeks in Egypt.

The example of *Dhoom 3* demonstrates that the categories of analysis used by producers and distributors in the Bombay industry do not work with Arab audiences. According to Ganti's field surveys, producers tend to favor an analysis of audiences in terms of a division between two Indias, one urban, the other rural, qualified by the grid of three city categories: A, B, or C, where the category A city—the major metropolis—overlaps with the overseas audience. Depending on whether the target audience lives in a category A, B, or C city, they will not like the same films. Subsuming the category of overseas under that of urban India, Indian producers tend not to be able to think of the market outside the dichotomy: diaspora/non-diaspora, which overlaps with the antagonistic couple, traditional/non-traditional market. However, Arab-speaking audiences do not fit so easily into this binary distinction between traditional (diaspora) and non-traditional (non-diaspora) markets, since they have been used to seeing Indian films for several decades and have a certain prior knowledge of commercial Hindi films, unlike audiences in Western Europe or North America, for example.

The Middle East, unlike the Emirates where South Indian cinema is a serious rival to Bollywood, remains for the moment a relatively virgin territory for Indian cinema and opens up a new market for Yash Raj Films where it can present itself as a powerful alternative to Hollywood hegemony. Yet, the stereotypes associated with Bollywood productions do not encourage regional distributors to take the risk of releasing Indian films. What's more, the relationship with Indian films in the Arab world is one of ambiguity, as Viola Shafik points out (Iordanova 2006). The perception and reception of these films is deeply ambivalent—popular with audiences, they are also discredited and contested. The convergence of Arab and Indian sensibilities lasted only a few years. At the end of the 2000s, as a more proactive strategy was put in place to bring Indian films to Arab-speaking audiences, the gap between the era of the first Indian successes (the 1950s), their exponential popularity in Egypt in the 1980s, and the present day really began to widen. The obstacles faced by YRF in its transnational release of *Dhoom 3* in the Middle East is a sign of changing audiences. The multiplex culture marks the advent of a different type of cinema-going public and endorses a translation of practices in the consumption of Hindi films, away from cinema halls.

REFERENCES

Athique, Adrian. 2008. The Global Dynamics of Indian Media Piracy: Export Markets, Playback Media and the Informal Economy. *Media, Culture & Society* 30 (5): 699–717.

Grimaud, Emmanuel. 2003. *Bollywood Film Studio ou comment les films se font à Bombay*. Paris: CNRS éd.

Iordanova, Dina. 2006. Indian Cinema's Global Reach. *South Asian Popular Culture* 4 (2): 113–140.

Mingant, Nolwenn. 2010. *Hollywood à la conquête du monde : marchés, stratégies, influences*. 1 vols. Cinéma et audiovisuel. Paris: CNRS.

CHAPTER 17

When Bollywood Builds Dubai Filmic Imagery: Renewed Visions of the Arabian Peninsula

Abstract Since the groundbreaking Indian film *Sangam* in 1964, Bollywood has woven urban fantasies into its narratives, transporting audiences to glamorous locales worldwide. While cities like Paris and New York have been celebrated in celluloid, Dubai remained on the periphery of Bollywood's cinematic imagination. However, the grandeur of Dubai has increasingly captivated Bollywood, shaping the Emirate's visual narrative.

From outdated depictions to modern reinterpretations, Bollywood's portrayal of Dubai has evolved. Initially entangled with mafia narratives and Orientalist imagery, recent films like *Welcome Back* (2015) have transformed Dubai into a backdrop for comedic twists, reflecting a shift toward a more positive portrayal. This transformation aligns with Bollywood's commercial interests and its integration within Dubai, presenting the city-state as a tourist haven.

Through visually captivating sequences, Bollywood showcases Dubai's iconic landmarks, forging a symbiotic relationship between Bombay and Dubai, with Bollywood serving as a powerful ambassador for the Emirate on the global stage.

Keywords Bollywood • Tourism • Film imagery • Orientalist imagery • Dubai • Urban imaginaries

In 1964, *Sangam* marked a breakthrough in the creation of urban imaginaries in Hindi cinema by shooting long sequences abroad, taking viewers on a journey to "exciting" Europe as per the poster's promise. Since then, Bollywood has appropriated the imaginary world of many cities. *Love in Tokyo* (Chakravorty, 1966), *An Evening in Paris* (Samanta, 1967), *Namastey London* (Shah, 2007), and *New York* (Khan, 2009) are only a few examples of cities that Bollywood put into the spotlight. As Paris or New York are sprawling in the global production of images, Dubai remains on the margins of film urban imaginaries. Yet, the grandeur of this spectacular city inspires Bollywood. As Indian labor workers are physically building Dubai's skyscrapers, Bollywood is contributing to the building of the Emirate's visual grammar.

Visions of the Past: Ancient Arabia and Orientalist Imagery

While Dubai is branding a global image of wealth, probity, and modernity, Bollywood's representations of the Emirate relied on outdated visions and stereotypes. Bollywood films have depicted Dubai as the land of the mafia in a mix with Orientalist imagery. Initially, commercial Hindi cinema did not refer to the cities of the Arabian Peninsula by name: they existed on the screen within the larger whole of the Arab world.

"Lately, all roads lead to Arabia and the latest in the industry to join the desert caravan is the producer-director P. N. Arora," a film critic joked in the May 13, 1955, issue of *Filmfare* about the film *Hoor-e-Arab*. While we do not have access to the images themselves in their entirety, the heap of film titles that testify to the presence of Arabia in Hindi cinema seems to encourage this critic's sarcastic observation. Among the most evocative titles are: *Arab Ka Chand* (Moon of Arabia—Naseem Siddiqui, 1946), *Arab Ka Sitara* (Star of Arabia—Nanubhai Vakil, 1946), *Arab Ka Saudagar* (The Merchant of Arabia—S.D. Narang, 1956), and *Arab Ka Lal* (Red of Arabia—A. Shamsheer, 1964). Indefectibly represented as the fictional background of a mythical temporality, the Arabian Peninsula is essentially summoned as Ancient Araby, that "golden chapter of the legendary history of humanity, when angels reigned over the earth and men believed in the miracle."[1] Take, for example, H.S. Rawail's *Teerandaz* or *Ruksana*, produced in August 1954:

---
[1] About the film *Lal-e-Yaman* (Homi Wadia, 1933), in an advertisement in the *Bombay Chronicle* of September 24, 1933 (quoted in Thomas 2013, 43).

Meena Kumari, acclaimed as the star of the year, makes her return as an exotic Bedouin princess in Talwar Films' romantic comedy-musical, *Ruksana*. She teams up again with Kishore Kumar, her on-screen partner in the company's previous hit, *Ilzam*. Shammi, Madanpuri, Randhir, Amar and Sunder lead the star-studded cast of this film set in ancient Arabia. The story revolves around a fabulous princess who loves and hates the same man for whom she gives up her throne. (Filmfare 1954, 41)

The geographical anchoring in a specific city is less important than the creation of an exotic Arab atmosphere, capable of making people dream. As Hindi productions left the studios with the arrival of lighter cameras better equipped for outdoor sound recording, the Arabian Peninsula appeared in natural settings in 1983, in *Chor Police* by Amjad Khan.

RESTORING THE IMAGE OF A MAFIA CITY: ONGOING REDEFINITIONS OF THE IMAGINARY OF DUBAI—FROM *NAAM* (MAHESH BHATT, 1986) TO *WELCOME BACK* (ANEES BAZMEE, 2015)

The mafia is a large part of the world cinematographic imagination, with emblematic films such as Francis Ford Coppola's *The Godfather*. India's cinema, too, has taken up the trope of the mafia. Organized crime was even involved in the real production of Bollywood cinema. Haji Mastan, born Mastan Haider Mirza in 1926, became the first famous gangster in Bombay to produce films. He recruited and trained the most famous and sought-after figure of the Indian mafia in contemporary times: Dawood Ibrahim, who played a role in setting up circuits for Hindi films in Dubai. Known worldwide after the 1993 bombings in Bombay, the Dawood Ibrahim case illustrates the porous borders between organized crime and the world of cinema. His rise was not without resistance and led to a gang war that culminated in the murder of Dawood's brother. By avenging the death of his brother, Dawood Ibrahim is now more than ever in the sights of the Bombay police. He took refuge in Dubai, as the city-state had no extradition treaty with India at that time. This mafia context fueled the imagination of Dubai in Hindi cinema as the first Bollywood productions came to shoot in the city-state. Among the thirty or so Hindi films shot in the Emirate, the majority feature mafia stories. The city's image in Bollywood is very strongly linked to all forms of illegal trafficking and unscrupulous characters.

In the first Hindi films shot in Dubai in the 1980s, *Chor Police* (Amjad Khan, 1983) and *Naam* (Mahesh Bhatt, 1986), the criminal atmosphere of the city of Dubai is combined with the topos of an Islamicate universe (Bhaskar and Allen 2009). On the one hand, the scenarios of these two films stage the imaginary of an anomic city. In *Chor Police*, the main character, Dr. Singh, accused of a triple homicide, takes refuge in Dubai to escape the Indian police. Mahesh Bhatt's film, *Naam*, tells the story of a mother and her two sons, Ravi and Vicky Kapoor. A modest family, they must also deal with Vicky's indomitable character, who always ventures into fraudulent schemes. Ravi, on the other hand, works hard to provide for his family and compensate for his brother's foolishness. Seeing the thousands of Indians who leave the country to make their fortune in Dubai, Vicky is determined to emigrate there. His brother Ravi arranges for a visa and a ticket for him. Once in Dubai, Vicky does not give any more news to his family. In Dubai, nothing goes as planned for him: his papers turn out to be fake and he has been scammed about his promise of employment. To stay in the Emirate, he is forced to work for the international trafficker, Rana. More than a film about the mafia, *Chor Police* also offers a commentary on the working conditions of migrants to the Gulf.

On the other hand, the narrative of an anomic world is modulated to the visual grammar of a Muslim city. The iconic figuration of the mosque serves to locate and define the city of Dubai as soon as it appears on the screen. The opening credits of *Chor Police* run against a backdrop of nighttime aerial views of the city that are repeated over and over again from different angles: skyscrapers, silver sea, highways, and a lit mosque. In *Naam*, the younger brother flies to Dubai halfway through the film. The geographical displacement of the character and his arrival in another country are signified by the sequence of shots in the plane, then a shot in which "Dubai International Airport" is spelled out, and a mosque, with its minarets and domes, in the background. This visual transposition is accompanied by music with oriental tones. This is a visual convention of the journey in Arab-Muslim land that finds its filiation in the films shot in studios, thus maintaining a form of homogeneity in the representation of the different cities of the Arab space, and in which the cinematographic imaginary of Dubai melts.

And yet, if at both chronological ends of the films shot in the Emirate the mafia weaves the red thread between Bombay and Dubai, the scenarios and the visual grammar have been radically transformed in thirty years. From the dramatic atmosphere of *Naam*, the mafia is now treated in a comic mode in *Welcome* (Anees Bazmee, 2007) and *Welcome Back* (Anees Bazmee, 2015). In the *Welcome* series, we dive into the life of a mafia family in a parody of *The Godfather*. In the first episode, Uday Shetty, a mafia godfather, decides to find a husband for his sister. But no suitor wants to associate with a family that is steeped in trafficking. In *Welcome Back*, Uday Shetty and his partner Majnu Pandey decide to end their criminal activities. They want to become honest businessmen and settle down permanently in Dubai. Two female diamond cutters pretend to be royal heiresses in order to marry the two partners and live off them. Between the first films with a dramatic tone and the last ones that play on these mafia characters in a comic way, we can observe an evolution of the cinematographic discourse on the emirate as the Gulf countries become the main market for the films of the Bombay industry. Between 1986 and 2015, in fact, just as the city has radically transformed, so have its images in Bollywood. In the *Welcome* films, the pomp and luxury of a mafia living in huge, sumptuous mansions—echoing the visual imaginary of marvelous palaces from the Arabian Nights—prevails over the quasi-documentary images of Vicky's arrival in the city.

Bollywood's commercial logic, as its industry is integrated in Dubai, works to put forward a more positive image of the city-state, manufacturing the visual rhetoric of Dubai as a tourist postcard. This is coupled with an elision of the reality of Indian communities in Dubai, whether it is the older migration of merchant families or the more recent migration of migrant workers (Vora 2013).

Inhabiting the City: The Bollywood Paradox— Between Invisibility and Postcard Imaginaries

While immigrant workers from the Indian subcontinent have literally built Dubai, Bollywood is constructing a postcard cinematic geography of the city. Little represented on screen, the imaginary of Dubai in film was almost virgin territory in the 1990s; yet, with one of the largest Indian diasporas, the city is part of the imaginary and lived reality of Indians, whether they live in India or in the Gulf (Vora 2013). Director Farah Khan visually represents the Indian experience of the city in a musical sequence in her 2014 film *Happy New Year*, "Satakli."

The story of *Happy New Year* is simple: a group of Indian amateur dancers compete in an international competition held in Dubai, where nationalism and patriotism mingle with the stakes of athletic performance. In the musical sequence "Satakli," Dubai takes on the Indian colors. The Dubai Mall supports the Indian team, the water jets in its fountain are painted in the colors of the Indian flag, and the team creates a frenzy wherever it goes in the city. The claim on the fictional mode of the place of India and the Indian diaspora in the city of the Emirates then take a political dimension. This will of recognition is inscribed in the urban space, by occupying it and displaying the colors of the Indian flag, and the figuration of the name of the country on panels which hang in emblematic places of the city, in a game of reappropriation of the space. For the director, Farah Khan, "in this film, Dubai is not just a place but a character in its own right" (Nair 2013). This sequence, in which the entire city flies the colors of the Indian flag, can be seen as a vindication of the Indian presence in the city, a presence made up mostly of workers who have physically participated in the construction of the city. However, this Indian diaspora rarely appears in Hindi films shot in Dubai, including *Happy New Year*. As Rachel Dwyer rightly points out,

> Even Hindi cinema has a hierarchy in its diasporas. European and American diasporas are most often represented, while few images of others appear. The luxury and shopping malls of the Gulf States are, however, sometimes referenced, but tinged with a whiff of banditry (Anees Bazmee's *Welcome*, 2007), while the poor or the majority of South Asians in the Gulf are invisible. (Dwyer 2013)

Similarly, the heroine of *Naqaab* (Abbas-Mastan, 2007) tells another character in that film that she has changed jobs twelve times in six months. We see her dressed in the uniforms of her various jobs, most notably as a construction worker with jackhammer in hand. This image is intended to create a comic effect and underlines the complete absence of migrant workers in Bollywood images of the city of Dubai. This voluntary elision is part of the rhetoric of a tourist iconography of the Emirate. A convergence is taking place between the film and tourism industries, on which Dubai is playing to the full. The Emirate relies on a real marketing strategy to promote tourism via Bollywood: the construction of the first Bollywood theme park in the world aims to attract the Indian population to Dubai (AFP 2016). Conversely, Bollywood creates tourist postcard images for the city.

The mall is an essential tourist attraction in Dubai and occupies a large part of the city's visual imagination. An architecture of modern urbanism, the mall incorporates an essentialized version of the "traditional" Islamic urban motifs of the souk (Fuccaro 2001). In Bollywood, it evokes the desire for consumerist modernity. A city of all possibilities, Dubai embodies a kind of El Dorado for Indian immigrants who dream of making their fortune there. In the first films, their dreams are shattered by the cruel reality of the city, in the following ones, the beauty of the splendor and luxury prevails over the underlying criticism. In *Lahoo Ke Do Rang* (Mehul Kumar, 1997), Akshay Kumar's character, on the edge of a highway in Bombay, imagines himself a millionaire: we then switch to another highway, in Dubai, in a luxury car that contrasts with the scrolling rickshaws in India. During this musical sequence, scenes are shot in the City Centre of Dubai, where the characters dance around indoor fountains and conveyor belts, a joyful mix of technological modernity and traditional architecture. They sing along to the lyrics that valorize consumer society and whose refrain sums up the essence: "I've earned my money, I've earned my love. I'm gonna buy a house and a car."

In Bollywood, the city is not shown but traversed, to use Dominique Noguez's formula (quoted in Jonas 1994, 11) and the musical sequences sometimes take on the dimension of tourist advertisements in the form of animated postcards. The emphasis is placed on the representation of skyscrapers in the Emirate and on its emblematic towers, Burj al-Arab or Burj Khalifa. Bollywood images take up the architectural discourse of the city while insisting on its beautiful romantic creek, the one of Deira in particular. A convergence is taking place between the cinema and tourism industries, signaling a growing integration between Bombay and Dubai. Indian filmmakers were among the first to film in the Emirate, and thus contributed to shaping the image of the city in India, but also, in part, internationally, within the Bollywood broadcasting circuits abroad. Thanks to Bollywood's international broadcasting power and the spectacular dimension of its films' images, Dubai benefits from a media and tourist influence and makes Bollywood one of the main ambassadors of the Emirate.

References

AFP, Dubai. 2016. Bollywood, Hollywood Enrolled in Dubai Tourism Drive. *Gulf Times*, June 6, 2016. http://gulf-times.com/story/497049.

Bhaskar, Ira, and Richard Allen, eds. 2009. *Islamicate Cultures of Bombay Cinema*. New Delhi: Tulika Books.

Dwyer, Rachel. 2013. Bollywood's Empire. Indian Cinema and the Diaspora. In *Routledge Handbook of the South Asian Diaspora*, ed. Joya Chatterji and David A. Washbrook. Londres/New York: Routledge.

Filmfare. 1954. Filmfare. *Filmfare*, April 2, 1954.

Fuccaro, Nelida. 2001. Visions of the City: Urban Studies on the Gulf. *Middle East Studies Association Bulletin* 35 (2): 175–187.

Jonas, Serge. 1994. Espaces et sociétés : revue critique internationale de l'aménagement, de l'architecture et de l'urbanisation/dir. publ. Serge Jonas. Paris: Éd. Anthropos.

Nair, Sangeetha. 2013. Shah Rukh Khan Enjoyed Shooting for 'Happy New Year' in Dubai. *The Times of India*, September 14, 2013. https://timesofindia.indiatimes.com/entertainment/hindi/bollywood/news/Shah-Rukh-Khan-enjoyed-shooting-for-Happy-New-Year-in-Dubai/articleshow/22580678.cms.

Thomas, Rosie. 2013. *Bombay before Bollywood: Film City Fantasies*. The SUNY Series, Horizons of Cinema. Albany (États-Unis): SUNY Press.

Vora, Neha. 2013. *Impossible Citizens: Dubai's Indian Diaspora*. Durham/Londres: Duke University Press.

CONCLUSION

Finally, at the end of this study on the circulation of Indian films in the Middle East, we can offer a belated response to Georges Sadoul and challenge the idea of a form of an innate affinity for Hindi films in the Arab countries. This preliminary work, which focused on the conception of the Arab space as a territory of distribution by the Bombay film industry, on the modalities of distribution, and on the networks that structure the dissemination of films, aimed to grasp, in their global dimension, the plural dynamics of the circulations at work. These dynamics have encountered forces of resistance as well as Hindi films' attempts to "conquer" theaters in the Arab space. One of the central questions underlying this work is how cinema constructs the Arab perception of the Indian world and vice versa. How does the Bombay film industry view the Arab world as a place to showcase its films? How, in the cities and countries studied, is Hindi cinema mobilized, thought of, and perceived, by the agents of its diffusion? Focusing on the perceptions of the actors of the diffusion on both sides, leaving aside an analysis of reception and of audiences, has allowed us to go beyond a sender/receiver relationship and reveal a complex network at work behind the circulation of cinema.

Thus, giving a voice to the actors of these little-studied circuits allowed me to argue against the widespread and essentializing idea of a passive

Arab public faced with its fascination for Bollywood. Returning to the processes of circulation in themselves opened the door to the asperities, the stumbling blocks of the narrative of these disseminations. In the hollow of these stumbling blocks, one of the fundamental characteristics of these networks emerges: their plasticity. The films circulate according to local conditions, be it structural (state of the film industry), legal, economic, and according to technological changes. If Hindi films have almost deserted cinema halls in Egypt and Lebanon and are mostly only accessible on cable and satellite channels, or on the Internet, they exist simultaneously on a plurality of mediums in Dubai: theaters, cable and satellite channels, VOD (Video on demand). Each country forms its own ecosystem for Hindi films. Thus, by returning to the historical dimension of the circulation of Hindi films in the region without restricting ourselves to the paradigm of Dubai, it is possible to note a form of amnesia on the part of the Bombay industry in relation to the distribution of its films in this territory. This work allows us to recompose a form of "memory" of the Bombay industry vis-à-vis the Middle East.

At the end of this work, the geographical and historical journey has led us to conclude that the exhaustion of the cinema network for Hindi films in Egypt and Lebanon has been matched by the rise of a rich ecosystem in the Emirates. In parallel to the observation of the mutations in circulation, the landscape of Indian film production has itself changed enormously. New Indian production companies such as Sikhya Entertainment and Phantom Films have helped to renew the independent Hindi film scene. These films have managed to find their place on the screens of multiplexes in India and a resonance in other countries, notably in France. While Bollywood and Kollywood are now well established in Gulf cinemas, will there be distributors willing to offer these different films in the Middle East, helping to change the perception of Hindi films for Arab audiences?

The Gulf environment offers a heuristic field of research for the current presence of Indian cinemas, by the plurality of networks and actors mobilized in various types of circulations, contrasting with the meager circulations of Hindi films in other countries of the Arab space. In this respect, working on the circulation of Hindi films within the framework of a transnational perspective and on the scale of several countries allows us to highlight a network of cinematic exchange that draws both links and borders between territories. Looking at the Middle East from the Bombay industry offers a new perspective and contributes to the complexity of the ecosystem of cultural industries in the region. While the notion of the avant-garde in cinema is largely reserved for its aesthetic and formal use and to designate "creators," those who bring films to life on the big screen are often perceived as playing only a secondary role as intermediaries. Taking the form of a historical anthropology of cinema, this work wanted to restore the avant-garde power of these precursors and pioneers of cinematographic circuits.

Index[1]

A
Aan, 26, 38–45
'Abdin, Hourriya, 102–105, 103n5, 105n8, 132, 133n2

B
Bilimoria, Manchersha B., 22–24, 27, 29–33, 40
Bollywood
 Hindi films, 4–7
 Indian cinema, 4–7

C
Chandni Chowk, 48–55
Chopra, B. R., 45, 49, 50, 52–54, 58–61, 113
Chopra, Yash, 112, 113, 148, 149
Cinema
 Femina-Paris, 41, 42
 Miami, 41–43
 Pigalle, 78, 86, 87
 Rivoli, 86, 112
 Shubra Palace, 97–106

D
Diaspora, 123, 151, 152
Diaspora market, 146–151
Distributor
 Egypt, 44, 81, 100, 101, 119, 132–138, 162
 India, 23, 27, 78–80, 105, 110
 See also under individual names

E
el-Sabban, Mohammad Khalid, 86

F
Festival, 134n4, 137

---

[1] Note: Page numbers followed by 'n' refer to notes.

G
Golchin, Ahmed, 142–144, 143n1, 152

H
Hinduja, 70–75, 72n3, 74n5, 78

J
Jumani, 76–81, 79n2, 79n4, 80n5, 80n6, 80n7, 80n8, 81n9
Jumani, Ranchor, 78–81, 84
Jumani, Sanjay, 78–81, 84

K
Kapoor, Raj, 15, 44, 70–75, 86, 89, 98, 133, 143
Khan, Mehboob, 40, 44, 70, 71, 86, 119, 133, 143

L
Lal-e-Yaman, 23, 30, 168n1

M
Mard, 103, 104, 106, 110–116
MBC Bollywood, 136
MENA
   MENAP, 124, 124n4
Merchants
   gold, 143
   Sindhi, 13, 66–69, 73
Mother India, 2, 44, 45, 70, 119, 133, 143
Movietone, Wadia, 23, 30, 91

N
Naaz, 67

O
Orientalism, 48–49, 53–55
   See also Orientalist imagery
Orientalist imagery, 49, 168–169
Overseas, 72

P
Panesar, Avtar, 144, 151
Policy
   foreign, 38, 45
   Indian, 7, 38
   state, 98
Politics, 4, 61, 92, 145
   See also Policy

S
Sangam, 11, 15, 44, 69–76, 86, 89, 98, 118, 133, 143, 168
Singh, Gurmuk, 24, 44, 80, 105
Skandar, Wajih, 44
Sobhi, Badiʿ, 81, 97–106, 102n2, 133, 133n2, 134, 136
Subtitles, 43, 80–81, 137, 152

T
Transnational circulation, 12, 13, 67, 72, 79–80

Y
Yash Raj Films (YRF), 13, 144, 148–156, 160, 162–165

Z
Zee
   Zee Aflam, 120–126, 121n3, 124n5, 125n6, 136
Zeind, Antoine, 132–138, 138n15, 161, 162, 164

SPRINGER NATURE

GPSR Compliance

The European Union's (EU) General Product Safety Regulation (GPSR) is a set of rules that requires consumer products to be safe and our obligations to ensure this.

If you have any concerns about our products, you can contact us on ProductSafety@springernature.com

In case Publisher is established outside the EU, the EU authorized representative is:

Springer Nature Customer Service Center GmbH
Europaplatz 3
69115 Heidelberg, Germany

The manufacturer's authorised representative in the EU is Springer Nature Customer Service Centre GmbH, Europaplatz 3, 69115 Heidelberg, Germany. If you have any concerns regarding our products, please contact ProductSafety@springernature.com

Printed and bound by CPI Group (UK) Ltd, Croydon, CR0 4YY

26/03/2026

02078942-0001